THE BIBLE AND CONTEMPORARY CULTURE

THE BIBLE
AND
CONTEMPORARY CULTURE

GERD THEISSEN

TRANSLATED BY DAVID E. GREEN

FORTRESS PRESS
MINNEAPOLIS

THE BIBLE AND CONTEMPORARY CULTURE

Cover design: The Design Works Group, Charles Brock
Cover image: Shutterstock
Book design: Josh Messner

Library of Congress Cataloging-in-Publication Data

Theissen, Gerd.
  [Zur Bibel motivieren. English]
  The Bible and contemporary culture / Gerd Theissen ; translated by David E. Green.
     p. cm.
  Includes bibliographical references and index.
  ISBN-13: 978-0-8006-3863-4 (alk. paper)
  ISBN-10: 0-8006-3863-8 (alk. paper)
  1. Bible—Criticism, interpretation, etc. I. Title.
  BS511.3.T46 2007
  220.6—dc22
                            2006026180

The paper used in this publication meets the minimum requirements of American National Standard for Information Sciences—Permanence of Paper for Printed Library Materials, ANSI Z329.48-1984.

Manufactured in the U.S.A.

10 09 08 07   2 3 4 5 6 7 8 9 10

CONTENTS

PREFACE

nyone who works with the Bible professionally as a scholar, as I do, or as a clergy or lay leader of a faith community has little occasion to wonder about the Bible's motivating power. After all, for such people, the Bible is the element in which they exist. They live, breathe, and think the Bible every day. It's hard for them even to imagine that anyone else might *not* have an interest in engaging the Bible. Scholars like me try to elicit a meaning from the original historical context of a text, and trust that this will somehow be transformed into an engaging message that relates to life today. But that transformation is hardly a matter to be assumed!

At the outset we must ask, *Which Bible* are we talking about? Or, in other words, *Whose* Bible is this, anyway? We hear very diverse claims for "ownership" of the Bible:

- As *a confessional document,* the book of a particular creed, the Bible belongs to the churches. In every church, a Bible lies on the pulpit or altar or communion table as a visible symbol of the community's confidence that this book offers an opportunity to come into contact with God.
- As *a text for preaching,* it authorizes personal and communal decisions and commitments and serves as a foundation for theology.
- As *a book for meditation* in private life, either in the forms of readings or "thoughts for the day," it also promises the reader an encounter with God.
- As *a text that often leads a hidden life,* its language swims up in the everyday stream of consciousness: for example, "the Lord is my shepherd; I shall not want..." or, when a wrong act calls up the words, "forgive us our trespasses as we forgive those who trespass against us...."
- As *a reference work,* the Bible often functions in contemporary society as the subject of teaching and scholarly investigation, not just in theology and religious studies but in art history and literature, history and ethics. All through the centuries it has been the inspiration for

painters, sculptors, and composers, and it still inspires great artists today. When a scholar encourages someone to study the Bible, he or she is often thinking of the Bible as a cultural artifact.

But in all these ways and more, the Bible remains *a thoroughly stubborn book*. Many ideas in it defy any churchly application. The person who approaches the Bible expecting to be edified will often be disappointed. And as material for education and betterment, it resists easy appropriation.

Today we have particular reasons for wondering just how the Bible should be appropriated, and why. What kinds of knowledge and expertise do we wish to pass on to future generations? For what purposes? In what selection and order? For a long time people could simply assume as an undisputed fact that succeeding generations *had* to gain familiarity with the Bible as a "great book" of our culture and civilization (as well as the foundation for faith). Nowadays that cannot be assumed, and the claim itself requires substantiation. Whether we are discussing the education of children or university students, the individual's striving for self-improvement, or relevance in the mass media, the question arises: *Why consider the Bible?*

This book is about that question. Though I approach the question from my own experience as a biblical scholar and teacher of the Bible in a university setting, I do not presume that my readers come from a religious background where the reading of the Bible is taken for granted; nor will I try to convince a nonreligious reader that they "ought" to care about the Bible for religious reasons. My question throughout will be, What *in the Bible itself* commends it to our careful attention? If that question meets with an attitude of open and curious inquiry in my reader, I will be satisfied.

I dedicate this book to Professor Hartwig Thyen, a colleague of many years, who has pleaded all his life for a love of the Bible both as a foundational text for faith and as an impressive body of literature.

INTRODUCTION

W hy should anyone read the Bible, let alone devote time to studying it? For religious-minded people who are accustomed, even devoted, to Bible reading, that question may seem nonsensical and even impertinent. *Of course* one should read the Bible! But that view is hardly self-evident. Many other people will never pick up the book if the only reasons to read the Bible depend on first holding religious beliefs *about* the Bible. Is it possible to commend the Bible on its own, apart from religious preconceptions about it?

The Bible remains part of the cultural bedrock of Western society, yet many people lack any sense that it is something with which they should be familiar if they don't happen to encounter it as a text for a sermon. This book addresses the question, Why should people who consider themselves educated study the Bible, even if biblical faith means nothing in their own lives? Why, if we lose our knowledge of the Bible, are we losing something irreplaceable?

I hasten to add that even within Christian churches—where one might expect the importance of Bible study to be a foregone conclusion—the Bible is in dispute. To attach immense importance to it is often taken to be the sign of a conservative, even fundamentalist, mentality. If, in conversation, someone pleads for a "Bible-based" viewpoint or claims a position "true" or "faithful to Scripture," we often suppose that person is expressing a conservative resistance to "the spirit of the age." (Ironically, we usually don't expect such a plea for a "biblical" viewpoint to express a prophetically inspired opposition to the status quo!)

Devotion to the Bible is weakest in the liberal traditions of the educated middle classes, for whom the Bible may be regarded as no more than part of the cultural baggage of their parents' or grandparents' generations. Appealing to such people to take the Bible seriously can mean asking people who think of themselves as politically progressive and intellectually critical, who consciously oppose religious conservatism, to care about the Bible as much as the religious conservatives do!

Even within the churches, then, what were once established reasons to read the Bible can no longer be taken for granted. Traditionally, the Bible is at the center of personal faith for Protestant Christians. But today even Protestants often look to other sources to provide the resources for faith: to art and literature, for example, or to philosophy, liturgy and spirituality, personal and social ethics, or meditation. Protestants can welcome closer ties with Catholicism and the new discovery of the Bible among Catholics, but it remains the case that the Bible suffers a diminished status even among Protestants. For Catholics and Protestants alike, the challenge today is to make the Bible's importance comprehensible in an increasingly secular world. Further, both Catholics and Protestants are challenged to rethink their understanding of the Bible's significance in dialogue with other religions. After all, Jews and Muslims appeal to the Bible, too, and Buddhists and Hindus have their own ideas about it, not to mention atheists! We all have something to learn from one another. But it is often in discussion with other religions that Christians are impelled for the first time to think critically about their own assumptions and traditions.

In formal theological scholarship, where one might turn for help in making a case for the Bible's importance, serious thinking about the Bible is generally put forward in the formidable language of "hermeneutics," that is, an often abstract theoretical understanding about the nature of interpretation itself. Biblical hermeneutics tries to answer the question, How can a text that came into being in the remote past still claim intelligibly to have validity for us? But framed theoretically in that way, hermeneutics is often far removed from real-life reading of the Bible. It doesn't touch on the situations in which men and women actually read and try—and, sometimes, fail—to make sense of the Bible every day. It is these everyday, practical situations that I have especially in mind in what follows, though I also intend to ask the fundamental questions about why the Bible matters.

Many clergy and teachers of religion feel that they are swimming against the tide. Throughout Europe and North America, we are experiencing an ongoing *secularization*. Though statistically Americans remain a religious people, telling pollsters that they believe in God and go to weekly worship services, it is also true that the proportion of Americans answering these questions in this way continues to decline year by

Introduction

year—and that biblical literacy is increasingly rare even among those who describe themselves as devoutly religious. The startling paradox in contemporary Western culture is that, on the one hand, secularization, especially in successful secular democratic states, has displaced the Bible from its former role in Christendom as a blueprint for religion, the social order, and cosmology. At the same time, under the pressures of the values of consumerism that inhere in the modern capitalist market, religion itself is increasingly privatized, so that Bible reading—or, in the language of some more evangelical churches, "getting into the Word"—is increasingly a matter of personal preference and individual endeavor. Both forces—secularization and the expansion of privatized religion—effectively exclude the Bible from its prior role as the premier commonly held cultural resource. The result is a proliferation of ways to read the Bible, some of them quite idiosyncratic.

What sometimes seems to be secularization may also be seen as an increasing *pluralism* of religious—and nonreligious—perspectives. There is an increasing *breadth* of the forms and expressions of religious experience, but that does not necessarily translate into spiritual *depth*. The mainstream churches, which put a particular value on an openness to diverse religious perspectives, find it difficult to bind people to them with the same strong sense of affiliation that more conservative churches, which readily offer certainty around a single normative perspective, enjoy. Meanwhile, so-called mega-churches continue to grow, and nondenominational "community" churches that identify themselves as simply "Bible-centered" thrive. These congregations offer more certainties, especially about the Bible's importance, but do not always yield a depth or breadth of understanding about the biblical witness or a respect for its historical distance from us.

Religious groups outside Christianity are also growing, so that some people talk about a return to religion or a resurgence of religion. Although the end of religion has been prophesied for at least two hundred years, it hasn't yet happened. More than a century ago Friedrich Nietzsche proclaimed that "God is dead," meaning the *biblical* God; but Gregory Tabori's answering quip has just as much validity today: "God says, 'Nietzsche is dead.'" Religion continues, but often as a shadow of secularization; as uncommitted Christianity; or as a conventional cultural religiosity within a mainstream church. It lives, even among people who consciously see themselves as citizens of this modern world. It lives on in a longing for the wholly Other, which will always drive the restless hearts of men and women, within or outside of organized religious communities.

The challenge within this wide spectrum of religion *and* irreligion, of simultaneously increasing religious pluralism *and* secularism, is to increase general awareness of what the Bible itself offers. On one hand, this challenge is intensified by the pressures of secularization and of what in the American context is routinely called the "separation of church and state," which means that those who regard the Bible, from a faith stance, as their primary resource for religious, ethical, and, yes, political questions often feel marginalized, pushed to the fringe of public life, and excluded. When they seek, for example, to integrate the Bible into a general curriculum of religious studies in public high schools and state universities, they often are met with great resistance from their fellow citizens who oppose what they perceive as an effort to impose the sort of indoctrination that is more appropriate in a private religiously-affiliated school. Even when the Bible is taught in the religious studies curricula of public schools, teachers know they must walk a thin line between conveying an enthusiastic appreciation for the contents of the Bible and appearing to advocate a particular religious posture.

On the other hand, when a similar dilemma is felt within more liberal churches, where people champion inter-religious understanding and dialogue yet also wish to respect the separation of church and state by constraining religious discourse in public schools and in the public square, the result can be an insipid Christianity that effectively insulates the Bible from having any dramatic influence in public life. In such churches, to speak about the Bible is sometimes to raise a yawn. But that tells us more about those churches than about the Bible itself!

My concern is not with how conservative or liberal churches fare, but with how the Bible fares in public consciousness. The sort of increase in biblical literacy that I have in mind will calmly pursue its own aim— explaining the importance of the Bible for the widest possible public, both through public institutions of higher education as such and through faith communities, so as to give the Bible its due in the public square. Promoting biblical literacy in this sense means giving an account of the Bible's significance to future generations as well as to the current generation. Opinion polls show that as a book for children the Bible is a solid success, but that adolescents view it as mainly important for the elderly and for people with problems. It does not immediately rouse their interest (though such could be said of many other subjects, so this is hardly a reason to stop working with biblical texts with high school students, of course!).

Unfortunately, too often claims for the Bible's significance are avoided even in the religious-studies classroom. From her experience training teachers, one colleague has put together the following list of arguments *against* teaching the Bible in public schools, which seems applicable to students at all levels:

- The Bible is a book belonging to the ancient world,
- without any importance for contemporary everyday life,
- only comprehensible by specialists,
- containing a patriarchal picture of God;
- by extolling a suffering figure it promotes a false readiness for sacrifice;
- its belief in God contravenes a life shaped around the individual's own value and thus is an obstacle to the psychological and emotional development necessary to individuation;
- it promotes the necessity of retaliation rather than reconciliation;
- it belongs to a superseded sabbatarian culture;
- it is full of improbable and untrue stories, and
- it is unsuitable as a book for children.

Accounts like this confirm the impression that the modern world is devaluing traditions like the Bible faster and faster. Of course, the very acceleration with which traditions are now cast aside has a paradoxical effect: the older the traditions, the less they are drawn into the vortex of modernization. The world of ideas we encounter in ancient Jerusalem and Athens appears "outmoded" more slowly than the most up-to-date notions from the centers of intellectual fashion. Consequently, the first question that arises as we approach the Bible—How does it commend itself to twenty-first-century generations?—is perhaps more easily answered than the question of which works of modern literature we should pass on to our children. How can the Bible be a part of lively conversations through which young people seek to discover their own identities? Don't the young need conversation with older people who approach life's existential questions from a position that goes beyond the minimum consensus of an open society, people who can speak with eloquence to their own convictions about values?

The answer to all these questions must be sought in the Bible itself. As young people often remind us (though their elders are probably at least as aware of the fact), "the Bible is an *ancient* book." Indeed, biblical scholars are as aware of that fact as anyone: after all, we know something about the past world from which it comes! Moreover, we are practiced in *respecting* that world and in avoiding the unwitting projection of it into our own. But the question is not simply whether the Bible is *old,* even ancient. The question is whether its very antiquity provides a valuable resistance to our modern world of ideas. Was it not one of Israel's great gifts to humanity to have created a canon that saved many subversive ideas from being forgotten?

The plea for a renewed public interest in the Bible may also be justified in terms of our shared political life. Because the Bible is often wielded in the crudest one-dimensional ways by political leaders who expect in this way to win support for their own understanding of "moral values," it is all the more important to promote a critically aware and socially responsible literacy regarding the central themes and resources of the Bible. Meanwhile, mainstream churches and allied faith communities and parachurch organizations that seek a proper role in influencing public policies from the perspective of their faith traditions rightly ask: Don't we need an honest and vibrant discussion of the social and moral values that derive from the biblical writings? Even if the minimum consensus in society consists in values we approve—individual responsibility, the inviolability of human dignity, human solidarity, reverence for nature—is that enough? Ought we not to be familiar as well with the biblical stories behind these slogans: responsibility as answerability *to God,* the dignity of men and women as appropriate to their being created *in God's image,* regard for others and for the earth as responsibility *to God's commandments* regarding love of neighbor and stewardship of creation? In short, without introducing the advocacy of any particular religious posture into public discussion, do we not have good reasons to claim that our society ought to be concerned with the Bible as a foundational text of our civilization and culture, even in places where it is no longer listened to as the text for a sermon?

Introduction

The present intellectual situation is favorable for reconsidering the question of the Bible's place in public life. We are increasingly aware that we live in a *post*-secular world in which, in the long run, religious people and nonreligious people must get along together. Traditional and traditionalist religions cannot recapture modern society, nor can secular intellectuals hope that religion is going to wither away. The two groups must learn to practice openness to one another. The postmodern mentality that has spread since the 1980s makes this easier. In architecture, this has meant that irreconcilable styles came to be accepted side by side as equally valid forms; in science, it has meant a healthy skepticism about absolute claims to an objective knowledge of reality. The "great narratives" have become discredited. And religion has changed as well: for if religion is but one more phenomenon in the modern world, "enlightenment" might mean understanding religion better than religion understands itself. There would be nothing particularly enlightened about expecting religious men and women to understand and accept the secular world while that world refused to enter into a respectful dialogue with them, preferring instead to offer only criticism and derision of religious conviction. Even for postmodern thinking, of course, religions present difficulty: they provide ultimate answers, they offer "great narratives," they maintain (or at least once maintained) absolute claims.

When in the following pages I argue for an open, public appreciation of the Bible that aims to make the Bible comprehensible to *everyone*, the appropriate context in which such an appreciation can grow is what critical theorist Jürgen Habermas has termed post-secular society. Up to now, any Bible teaching that included its *religious* content was bound to be understood as an attempt at missionizing or proselytizing on the part of the churches. A postmodern mentality can more easily enter into the convictions of other people without feeling pressured to agree with them. It can express convictions without advocating those convictions from a missionary stance.

READING THE BIBLE DIFFERENTLY FROM FUNDAMENTALISTS

The approach I have in mind is necessarily distinguished from that of Christian Fundamentalism (as defined in a series of twelve volumes published between 1910 and 1915)[1], which reacts to the present situation in a diametrically opposite way. Fundamentalism must be distinguished from traditional pietism, which had its roots in the seventeenth and eighteenth centuries, and for which the essentials were conversion, a turning to Jesus, and practical expressions of faith in terms of charitable acts benefiting one's neighbor. This pietism often turned against the church as institution and rejected an orthodox theology remote from life. Its focus on inner experience was a distinctly modern element. Fundamentalism, on the other hand, as it originated in North America and continues to flourish there, is a reaction against an increasingly secularized politics as well as against the modern science and scholarship of the nineteenth century. The Niagara Creed of 1878 listed four christological "fundamentals," in addition to the verbal inspiration of Scripture. These were the Virgin Birth, Christ's vicarious death, his bodily resurrection, and his second coming. But three other concerns were much more decisive:

1. Rejection of historical-critical research into the Bible, that is, rejection of the general rational interpretation of the text.
2. A fight against the doctrine of evolution in favor of a creationism that interprets the Bible's account of creation literally and rejects human descent from apes.
3. The defense of traditional morality, especially in opposition to women's emancipation, abortion, and homosexuality.

Here I should also distinguish evangelicalism from Christian Fundamentalism. Evangelicals are, generally speaking, more moderate. They accept modern culture and maintain a broader, maximalist theology: as much as possible in the Bible is to be considered historical, and as much as possible of the church's creed is to be preserved. Here there is a deliberate avoidance of exaggerated Fundamentalist positions.

In the late 1970s and early 1980s there was a renaissance of the fundamentalist spirit in Christianity, as well as in Judaism and Islam, as indicated by four events in particular: the 1977 rise to power of the Likud Block in Israel; the 1978 election of Karol Wojtyla as Pope John Paul II; the 1979 return to Tehran, Iran, of the Ayatollah Khomeini; and the decisive support of Christian Fundamentalists in the 1980 election of Ronald Reagan as President of the United States. If pietism, with its emphasis on inner experience, is a phenomenon of the modern world, the same can be said of the new fundamentalism. Whereas postmodern thinking accepts pluralism and its relativization of certainties, fundamentalist thinking protests the dissolution of assured truths. Formally speaking, it is related to modernist thinking, which insists on objective scientific findings, generally acceptable moral judgments, and the force of progress. Fundamentalism also insists on objective religious truths, binding moral values, and an eschatological vision of salvation that applies to the whole world. The rise of a politically engaged religious right is an attempt to restore the lost, once-accepted validity of religion by means of political power, and aims to sell religion as a (pseudo-) modern product. In this vision, faith is supposed to be as firmly anchored in fact as any other scientific theory.

The outcome is a bitter struggle about who has the competence to interpret the Bible. For fundamentalism, historical-critical research is seen as the great opponent. Just as economic concerns can put up with no "heretics" who dissent from the general business philosophy, so fundamentalism endures no critics who call it into question. Moreover, just as our capitalist society judges theories according to their potential for a successful transformation into products, with the market functioning as the instrument for arriving at truth, so modern fundamentalism submits to a similar law. It wants to "sell" its "products" successfully, and with this aim employs the usual market strategies. Though it is antimodern in feeling, it appears on the stage in the distinctly modern dress of its invention, the electronic "church" of televangelism. It is antimodernism in modern guise.

Fundamentalist and evangelical groups claim the Bible emphatically for themselves. But the method for Bible study and teaching I am putting forward here is the opposite of that espoused by fundamentalism. It affirms historical-critical research, the evolutionary view of nature, and the need to examine moral norms—all values upheld in most Protestant churches. Yet in the Protestant churches, although the Bible is the agreed basis for the church and for ecumenical relations, holding high "the Bible" and the word *biblical* does not produce automatic consensus among Protestants. Both terms have become the shibboleths of evangelical groupings and are potentially divisive. Only a minority in the Protestant churches want to be "faithful to Scripture" in the sense of the evangelical slogan. Even the phrase "biblical teaching" often has unwelcome associations.

The open, public appreciation of the Bible that I advocate here uses the words *Bible* and *biblical* in a sense that runs counter to the general trend toward undervaluing the Bible in mainline Protestantism. I take heart from the fact that in Catholicism, since Vatican II, the Bible has become the symbol of a progressive theology, not least where it has been rediscovered in Latin American base communities. Even though within the established churches some Protestants are now engaged in a flight from the Bible, the influence of the Bible continues to be felt most strongly at the frontiers of the church—as has often been the case. The future of the Bible among Christians thus seems assured because of what is happening, for example, in the "emerging" church.

But the Bible does not belong only to Christians. The Old (or First) Testament is Judaism's book as well. In Islam, the twofold Bible of Old and New Testaments is the preliminary step to the complete revelation. The Bible has played a part in determining European and North American history far beyond the confines of the church, even when its influence has taken the form of criticism of the Bible and of religion. The scope of the adjective *biblical* is far wider than the dimensions of the words *fundamentalist, evangelical, Protestant, Catholic, church,* or *Christian*—hence my plea for an *open, public* study and appreciation of the Bible.

An open, public study of the Bible, intended for everyone, irrespective of belief or disbelief, is in accord with the Bible itself. Judaism was the first religion to create a canon, and by so doing it also created "the religion of the book" as a type. One can get acquainted with these book religions, such as Judaism, Christianity, or Islam, without subjecting oneself to their ritual and ways of life—without eating kosher meals, making a pilgrimage to Mecca, or attending Mass—by reading their sacred texts. Whether or not one believes is another matter. But to *understand* these religions, one has only to read. It is true that the great book religions have a missionary element. But their books can be read independently of that. And in so doing the reader is in line with the motives that played a part in the emergence of the Bible.

When the Bible came into being, outsiders were in view. The Old Testament canon began to crystallize with Ezra, who (probably) at the beginning of the fourth century B.C.E. refounded the Jewish community on the instructions of the Persian king, taking as his basis "the law of the God of heaven" (Ezra 7). We do not know what this "law" was that he brought with him, but the intention was not merely to found an internal order but also to secure the autonomy of Judaism over against the outside world. The Persian rulers were prepared to respect this law. We come across a similar outward-looking function of the canon in the Septuagint, the ancient Greek translation of the Jewish Scriptures. According to the *Letter of Aristeas*, which describes the production of this translation, the Septuagint is an account of the Jewish religion intended for non-Jews. The translation was made for the famous library in Alexandria (*Aristeas*, 9f.). The letter depicts the translators in a long conversation with the Gentile king about the proper nature of government. Even if this is a legendary tradition, it shows that—irrespective of the real historical motives behind this translation of the Bible—from the Jewish viewpoint the Septuagint was not meant to be purely "insider" literature.

The New Testament, on the other hand, came into being solely as a response to impulses within the earliest Christian communities. It is the literature of small groups. For that very reason it is all the more astonishing that we should find in it what I call a "journalistic" thrust. That is, these earliest writings verge on a Christian journalistic impulse insofar as they purport to announce "the gospel," which means not just "good news," but joyful news with a decidedly *public* character. This public proclamation is the subject of the Epistle to the Romans, the first Christian writing to embody this "journalistic" impulse. In the first chapter of Romans, Paul names as his addressees *all the nations* (Rom. 1:16f.), Greeks and non-Greeks, the wise and the foolish (Rom. 1:14). This public proclamation of "good news" is also the theme of the earliest Gospel (Mark 1:1). It is to be spread throughout the world (Mark 13:10; 14:9). Though missionary intentions are of course behind this, the fact remains: the New Testament aims to be read by everyone, not just by believers. We have evidence showing that in the ancient world critics of Christianity were already studying it. So an open, public study of the Bible does not run counter to the Bible's own intentions.

In what follows we will ask: What should we look for in the Bible? What in the Bible will promote healthy dialogue with other people? In all that follows, I presume that no approach can do more for the Bible than it can do for itself. Ultimately people read the Bible because it has its own power to engage us. I realize that my own suggestions can do no more than help to call attention to this power to engage readers, so that they can find their own reasons for coming to know the Bible better.

CHAPTER 1

Why Any Educated Person
Should Know the Bible

Homer was the Bible of the Greeks. Even when they no longer believed in Homer's gods, they held fast to his epics. Even Christians read Homer. He remained part of humanistic and literary education after the collapse of the ancient world. Could the same thing happen to the Bible? Could it outlive its erosion as a source for interpreting the world and human life? There are hints that it might. Just as educated Christians continued to read Homer in late antiquity, in the modern era non-Christian intellectuals like Bertolt Brecht and Ernst Bloch read the Bible. But what value could the Bible have for people who no more believe in the incarnate Son of God than the early Christians believed in Homer's gods? What does knowledge of the Bible contribute to our awareness of history, to mastering problems in the present and future? And can such knowledge of the Bible enable dialogue with Jews and Muslims?

THE BIBLE'S CONTRIBUTION TO UNDERSTANDING REALITY

Our universe of knowledge has been divided into the natural sciences, the social sciences, and the humanities. Knowledge of the Bible belongs to the humanities but also bears on the other realms of knowledge. We will first explore how the Bible relates to each of these three forms of knowledge.

The Natural Sciences
It is common to refer to the knowledge gained by the natural sciences as dominating knowledge, because it enables human beings to control

natural processes through technology. The experimental origin of scientific knowledge through technological intrusion into nature makes this "instrumental" interpretation of the natural sciences plausible. Whatever knowledge comes through intrusion into nature can also help us intrude more effectively. But this is not all there is to scientific knowledge. The natural sciences also seek orientation concerning the world. We need knowledge of the elemental processes of nature, the structure of matter, and the origin of species in order to integrate ourselves realistically into the overall scheme of things. Here the natural sciences offer indispensable "orienting knowledge." Even if they cannot tell us what we should do in our place in the cosmos, at least they provide a realistic description of that place and help us better assess what we might do there. We are dependent on the natural sciences to develop our own self-conception, not just to dominate nature. To leave them out of the cultural canon is a mark of cultural illiteracy.

Here the Bible has a role to play. Scientific knowledge has displaced the biblical view of the world, but at the same time the biblical belief in creation has motivated our desire for scientific knowledge.

The emancipation of scientific curiosity from the constraints of the biblical worldview is part of the birth of the modern world. The primacy of knowledge over our desires—including the desire to rest secure in traditional interpretations of the world—has won the day. The Bible has lost its authority to explain the world. It has ceased to define the way things are.

And yet it would be too simple simply to contrast the biblical worldview and modern natural science. Myth is the initial attempt of reason (*logos*) to understand the world and assign human beings a place in it. The biblical creation story itself illustrates this, especially when we compare the (later) first account of creation (Genesis 1) with the second (Genesis 2). The first bears witness to wonder at the ordered sequence of the works of creation and the order established by God's decisions. It is a theory of evolution in mythological dress, in which human beings appear at the end and become aware of their responsibility for this world.

If a prescientific thirst for knowledge was already at work in early stages of the Bible, it is easier to understand that the subsequent history of the biblical belief in creation promoted scientific knowledge through two motivations: sensibility for wisdom and the contingency of nature.

1. Even today, wonder at the "intelligence" invested in the world gives the knowledge acquired by the natural sciences religious overtones. For Kepler, Newton, and many other scientists, a wonderful wisdom was concealed in nature. They read nature as a book written by God in the language of mathematics.
2. At the same time, knowledge of the world's contingency has motivated empirical research: everything about the natural world could be different if God had willed it so. No *a priori* idea can anticipate the order of nature: it can only be observed and described *a posteriori*. Even the experimental method converges with the biblical notion of creation: if God acted as a "technologist" in creating the world, it can best be known by following in God's footsteps—just as the work of a potter is best understood by someone who makes pottery.

Today belief in the wisdom and contingency of nature has outlived belief in God, in a kind of cosmo-religious piety in which scientific findings are emotionally inflated. But this response to science merely illuminates a strength of mythology that has been lost in the natural sciences: with all our knowledge, we still cannot assign ourselves any meaningful place in the universe. Science limits itself ascetically to the world as it is, ignoring questions of value or meaning. With all our knowledge, we can indeed understand nature far better than could the authors of the biblical creation account. But this knowledge leaves us unable to formulate the refrain that reechoes through the biblical account: "Behold, it was good."

Science and the Bible are linked by the history of science, an aspect of the natural sciences that belongs to intellectual history. For the natural sciences are human activities; they have a history. In order to understand the origin of our modern worldview, we must know the mythological world of the Bible, so as to understand how theological convictions have both motivated and restricted scientific knowledge, and to appreciate the integrative achievement of mythological thought that has been lost in the natural sciences: the interpretation of the world as something precious.

Such historical considerations lead to material links between the Bible and the findings of the natural sciences. On the one hand, scientific knowledge may be incorporated into belief in a creator who created (and continues to uphold) the world as the locus of human life. Then one can say something like this: God created matter in such a way that it contains within itself the power to evolve continuously into higher forms of organization. The seven days of creation of the biblical account are expanded into evolutionary stages. What actually took place in these stages is discoverable by science, but assessment of their worth is left to the praises of the Bible. Ernesto Cardenal has expressed this poetically in one of his Latin American psalms. I cite only the beginning here:[1]

> Bless the Lord, O my soul
> Lord my God you are great
>   You are clothed with the energy of atoms
>   as with a mantle
> From a cloud of whirling cosmic dust
> as on a potter's wheel
> you began to tease out the whorls of the galaxies
> and the gas escapes from your fingers condensing and burning
> and you were fashioning the stars
> You made a spatterdash of planets like spores or seeds
> and scattered comets like flowers....

Another possibility is to incorporate the emergence of the biblical religion within the framework of an evolutionary scientific interpretation of the world, with the evolutionary interpretation extended to human civilization, understood as the final stage of a comprehensive process. This approach raises the question: What role does religion play in this evolution? Have the social imperatives of religion set limits to the "struggle for life"? Sociobiologists face the riddle of how altruistic behavior in human civilization could be extended to genetically unrelated individuals. In biological evolution, altruistic behavior prevails only when it "pays"—that is, when it increases the probability of propagating one's own genes. In this context, the only altruism that pays is altruism that expects reciprocity or altruism toward those who are genetically related. Human ethics, however, demands that we help others whether they are related to us or not. This raises the question: Has religion with its inward power to control behavior enabled us to treat genetically unrelated people as our "brothers" and "sisters"? Has it, in combination with an empathy made possible by our cerebrum, led to an ethics designed to protect even what is biologically unfit? Is this how the principle of solidarity trumped the principle of selection? Just as in the transition from chemical to biological evolution the principle of entropy was suspended within a limited context, so the principle of natural selection might have been suspended in the transition from biological to cultural evolution. In this "anti-selectionist" view of human civilization, the Bible becomes central to civilization, for it is a protest against the principle of natural selection, which eliminates the weak and unfit. Even though such approaches are "experimental," they at least deserve mention.

In any case, the natural sciences are crucially important for the future of religion and criticism of religion. Postmodern relativization of the natural sciences may make valid points; it does not shape the thinking of people in general, however, but only of a few intellectuals. Today the natural sciences are rightly considered the most resilient form of knowledge. If we are to deal with human beings as they really live their lives we must take science more seriously than many theologians do.

The Social Sciences
The knowledge acquired by the social sciences is cooperative knowledge. It enables people to work with others and understand their behavior. Since this knowledge comes only through cooperation with others, its categorization as cooperative knowledge is plausible: the social sciences depend on people's willingness to respond to surveys and participate in experiments governed by certain rules. The cooperative knowledge so gained can be used in various ways: to manipulate or to emancipate, conservatively or progressively. It can help people dominate each other or expand the scope of their freedom. But here, too, it remains true that this knowledge plays an orienting role quite apart from any manipulative or emancipatory use. Psychology helps us understand the basic features of our thought, perception, and behavior; sociology helps us understand that our notions of the world and of morality as well our actions are socially conditioned. Both are important for our self-conception.

What role does the Bible play here? It is a book that guides religious communities as a normative quantity, a book with social power that has motivated both effectual "domination" imposed from above and protest from below. In the course of history, religion with its symbols has always been an instrument for both cooperation and aggression! It has been a source of social equilibrium and the occasion of hermeneutical—that is, interpretive—civil war.

This is true even for the emergence of rational behavior. It has roots not only in Greek and Roman antiquity, but in the Bible as well. It tells how the governance of life according to the commandments of the one and only God was practiced exemplarily by an entire people. In early antiquity, Jews were often considered a philosophical people. Philosophers were the only people who gathered around books and tried to live by what they taught. Here, however, an entire people was attempting to realize with absolute consistency a lofty ethos. They worshiped a God who was invisible and a blazing focus of ethical energy. Their enhanced devotion to ethical norms led to an increased sense of guilt—the downside of an intensified ethical sensibility. Self-discipline had its dark side. In Paul's writings we already sense a revolt against the oppressive aspects of the law. Modern critics of religion like Friedrich Nietzsche and Sigmund Freud have uncovered and analyzed this dark side of human self-repression. But the Bible's influence has produced not only criticism of religion but also a stream of blueprints by which even ordinary human beings have realized a consistent way of life, knowing that they can walk erect through life like kings.

But the Bible has not always simply promoted rational behavior and repression. It has also been a source of criticism and rebellion. One example may suffice: the *Hessische Landbote*, a pamphlet written in 1834 by Georg Büchner and the theologian Friedrich Ludwig Weidig, which is filled with biblical quotations and allusions:

> Peace to the hovels! War to the palaces! In the year 1834 it looks as though the Bible lied. It looks as though God created the peasants and workers on the fifth day and the princes and aristocrats on the sixth, and as though the Lord said to the latter, "Have dominion over everything that creeps upon the earth," classing the peasants and townsmen with the vermin.[2]

In the social sciences, too, the Bible can be viewed from two perspectives. Their findings can be set in a theological context. In this case the church is an entity based on experiences of transcendence; it cannot be derived from any social reality. But the social sciences can comprehend its earthly aspect in terms of communities, hierarchies, and structures.

Frequently, however, theological issues are set in the context of the social sciences. The result is often a scathing criticism of religion. Religion is viewed as regression to infantile dependence or as refusal to look harsh reality in the eye, because we need the loving father in heaven as an emotional safeguard. Or it is exposed as an expression of class conflict, either as an impotent revolt against oppression (and as the groaning of creation), or as a fetishistic glorification of dependence on self-created modes of production. This modern criticism of religion employs biblical metaphors and images. When Karl Marx speaks of religion as the "groaning of creation," he is borrowing a motif from Romans 8:22. His theory of fetishism chimes with the prophets' criticism of idols made by human hands (for instance, Isa. 44:9-20): in an idol, what human beings produce acquires numinous power over them and is worshiped as a deity. Freud thought of himself in terms of Moses, who had to lead a rebellious people into the desert. His god *Logos* has features of the Old Testament God.

Psychological and sociological interpretation of the Bible is also inspired by criticism of religion, but as a rule it does not share the same blanket value judgments. Therefore, it does not restrict itself to the trivial aspects of religion. Instead, its empirical analysis of what can be studied in the Bible reveals what is beyond analysis, like cracks in a wall. However the Bible and religion are categorized in their social setting, faith insists on the grounds of its own self-conception that it is not deducible from nonreligious factors. Even if it were in fact dependent, its defiant assertion of independence would have to be respected as oppositional autonomy—that is, as human revolt against the omnipotence of society. Even granted an extreme reductionism of religion to psychological and social processes, no one can deny that it consists of signs and symbols that aim to point beyond themselves. They must be interpreted as to their meaning. And that is the task of the interpretive humanities, to which we turn next.

The Humanities

What the humanities know about literary and material evidence is knowledge that enables us to understand each other; it promotes communication. Mastery of language is always the precondition for understanding. But mutual understanding is not just the object of the humanities but

7

also their precondition, without which they could not advance. Nevertheless, one cannot deny that the humanities have instrumental goals: languages are structures governed by rules, and linguistic competence is a kind of "knowledge of domination." It is not by chance that we speak of "mastering" a language. Mastery of language serves good as well as evil purposes, propaganda and enlightenment, truth and lies. But it is still true to say that we do not study the sources that document the past only for these purposes, but also as expressions of how human beings have understood themselves. We are interested in how people have mastered and interpreted their lives in order to gain insights into the ways we might do the same. As a rule, we interpret the sources with others and for others. In conversations about texts, we ask about possibilities for understanding ourselves in the present, possibilities on which we can agree. Our approach to the texts is often presented as though we had to heed the "call" of the past in our encounter with it. This approach turns every human self-concept into a *kerygma*, a message calling on us to change our lives. But it remains true that the understanding we gain through the humanities serves in the first instance for orienting ourselves to the possibilities for human life. Clearly, the Bible presents a distinctive way of life. It was uniquely put together in the life of a small nation as an attempt to interpret and master human life. In this sense it embodies an appeal that will always be heard. The Bible has left many traces of this appeal within the realm of the humanities, traces that must be deciphered even when the Bible has eroded as a foundation for life. For the study of history, for the study of art and literature, basic familiarity with the Bible is essential.

In the humanities, too, the two options already outlined are available: humanistic knowledge can be incorporated into a theological context (an option that poses no theological problems) or an attempt can be made to understand the theological context within a larger humanistic context.

Understanding the Bible is the archetype of all modern hermeneutics—that is, the principles of interpretative method. Interpretation was formerly governed by norms based on theological principles. Nowhere was the emancipation of interpretation from such normative principles a more sweeping drama than in the exegesis of the Bible. Only slowly was it accepted that rational methods must be used to study the Bible. At the same time, understanding of the Bible became the archetype of a preservative hermeneutics that sought to discover what could still be of use today despite the passage of time. There is good reason why we call any book that becomes authoritative for a particular group its Bible. When books are studied with existential involvement, the interpretation of the Bible stands as a model.

Conversely, however, the interpretation of the Bible can be accommodated to the methods of the humanities. The Bible can be analyzed using the general categories of religious studies. A "theory of the primitive Christian religion" can analyze it as a sort of "semiotic cathedral" constructed not with stones but with texts, metaphors and symbols, rituals and ethical norms. Just as very human motives led to the building of our cathedrals, so, too, with the semiotic cathedral of the biblical religion. But anyone who would understand more than a very little of it must respect its purpose: it was built for the worship of God, so that people could give expression to their relationship to transcendence. That is an external perspective on religion, which a "visitor" to this cathedral can share without taking part in its worship. But the visitor can be fully sympathetic toward those who dwell in the cathedral.

Contrary to the tendency of all forms of knowledge to stress only a specific pragmatic interest—domination of the natural world, cooperation, or mutual understanding—it must be emphasized once more that all knowledge serves first and foremost to orient. That function transcends any specific purpose. Without scholarly study we cannot develop an appropriate self-concept in this world, so we must consider all three branches of knowledge, within each of which the Bible has significance. In each we find a dual correlation with religion and the Bible. On the one hand, traditional theology may constitute the context into which scientific interpretations are incorporated. Since theology deals with the entire universe, whereas the various sciences are concerned only with partial aspects of it, this approach is in large measure plausible. Since the sciences deal only with facts, whereas theology looks for meaning, they can supplement each other. But also necessary, and in our modern culture inescapable, are attempts to integrate religious and biblical language into the context of the secular sciences. This approach ends in criticism of religion, but it also discovers the mystery of religion as a symbolic cultural language that promises vital benefit through relationship to an ultimate reality. Often it is only in this way that our modern civilization can approach religion and the Bible. Therefore, it is just as important as an approach based on a theological preconception that hopes to establish dialogue with God with the help of the Bible.

So far we have taken as our starting point the internal structure of knowledge organized into three broad realms. But more than simply having realms of knowledge opened up to them, people seek empowerment to master their lives. Therefore, we shall now turn to the contribution of the Bible to this mastery—not just for those who are religious, but for everyone.

UNDERSTANDING THE BIBLE AS A PATH TO UNDERSTANDING OURSELVES

The Bible remains an important document of our roots, regardless of whether it orients us for the living of our lives or merely reminds us of an age that is past. It is not easy to delineate this historical importance of the Bible briefly, but we shall present a few key ideas, without trying to be exhaustive.

Understanding a Common Past

All that we know about human history points to the Middle East as the place where human cultural evolution began to accelerate—the Fertile Crescent that includes Egypt, Syria, and Mesopotamia. Here we find the origin of the city, the state, and writing. Our modern history began with two small nations on the margin of this world that consciously set themselves apart from it, although they had deep roots within it: Israel and Greece.

The Israelites defined themselves by dissociation from the "house of bondage" in Egypt and the Assyrian foe to the north. They understood themselves as having been set free by their successful exodus from that old world. And yet Israel's Holy Scriptures preserve this world for us in a form that still lives today: its wisdom, its legal system, its prayers, and echoes of its myths. Religio-historical study can make the Old Testament sound as a symphony in which we can hear the themes and problems of long-vanished cultures. The Israelites enriched the concept of cultural memory though the notion of a canon, a collection of writings in which they withdrew their retrospections from the treacherous memories of human beings. In the process, they developed a culture of learning and remembering that to this day has shaped our approach to the past, especially where guilt and failure must be dealt with. In these writings:

1. They inscribed on our culture an *image of humanity* that ascribes to each individual, made in the image of God, an inviolable dignity. This image lives on in the inviolability of human dignity, even where the premise behind it has eroded.
2. They formulated an impressive *mandative ethics*, by making the law of God—still alive today in the Decalogue and the command to love one's neighbor—independent of all human authorities.
3. They conceived a *vision of history* that makes human beings responsible for the course of events, but also drives them to repent and change course when it is necessary to turn away from a disastrous past.
4. Above all in these texts there bursts forth belief in the one and only God. There emerged an *understanding of God* that saw God as a focus of infinite ethical energy. When the modern world affirms or denies God, it means the God of the Bible.

We cannot imagine our history without the Bible's image of humanity, its ethics, its understanding of history, and its image of God. Every educated person must be familiar with these ideas.

The Greeks, by contrast, shaped their self-awareness through epics of the Trojan War and the history of their struggle for freedom against the Persians. They rebelled against the notion of foreign domination and were the first to design a form of democratic community in which people govern their own affairs. They developed an ethics of self-control for free people that makes plausible our ability to set limits on authority. And they produced a philosophy that subjected every premise about life to constant scrutiny—in competition among many schools and approaches.

Both Jews and Greeks hit on the belief in the one and only God at roughly the same time (in the sixth century B.C.E.): Xenophanes of Colophon among the Greeks, Deutero-Isaiah among the Jews. Both nations turned their backs on a long-familiar world in which they had deep roots. They engaged in intensive dialogue during the Hellenistic period. Primitive Christianity emerged from this dialogue, combining the Jewish ethics based on commandments with the Hellenistic ethics based on insight.

In primitive Christianity we find them joined in the form of a mandative ethics that seeks its foundation in insight, because God has set the divine commandments in the human heart. Paul applies the philosophical notion of "testing" to God's will. He commands: "Test everything; hold fast to what is good" (1 Thess. 5:21), and "Test what is the will of God" (Rom. 12:2). Here we also find the notion of a community in which all are free—even aliens, slaves, and women, who were not free elsewhere in the ancient world (Gal. 3:28). It is characteristic of this community that all should exercise their freedom in mutual service (Gal. 5:13-14). Here the notion of freedom comes from the Greek tradition of ethical autonomy, the notion of service to others from the Jewish tradition. Here we see the influence of the Jewish ethics that is centered on one's neighbor, which focuses not on the self-determination of the individual but on the needs of others. To this day, both traditions shape our ethics.

Communication in a Shared Present
A pluralistic world depends on people's ability to understand each other even when they disagree. Inability to speak and understand lays the groundwork for conflict—up to and including terrorism, whether its roots are religious or secular. Our assessment of the religious factor in the conflicts of this world has changed remarkably in recent years.

In the middle of the twentieth century, the primary threats to the history of the world were secular ideologies: National Socialism and Stalinism, racism and imperialism. The traditional religions appeared to be a bulwark of defense against their attacks. National Socialism was met by the protest of the Confessing Church; in Communist countries, the religious principles of the churches made them immune to Communist propaganda. Colonialism was met by nativistic movements as the forerunners of liberation movements. Prominent figures embodied the humane aspect of religion—people like Albert Schweitzer, Mahatma Gandhi, Martin Luther King Jr., and Dietrich Bonhoeffer. This picture changed toward the end of the century. Insoluble conflicts between Protestants and Catholics in Northern Ireland, between Christians and Muslims in Sudan, between Hindus and Muslims, Israelis and Arabs—all give the impression that religion motivates fanaticism and aggression. Religious leaders now include such unattractive and, to some, demonic figures as Ian Paisley, Ayatollah Khomeini, and Osama bin Laden. The inhumane potential of religion has surfaced. Its humanizing potential still comes to the fore in the peace movement, in provision of asylum, in aid for developing countries that is not organized by the state. But such actions receive far less attention than the outbreaks of religious fanaticism in war and terrorism.

In this situation, Western intellectuals should be able to see through knee-jerk reactions: for example, "since religion makes political conflicts insoluble, it is best to bid it farewell. Since this farewell to religion is now history, we are on the side of the righteous." But such reactions do nothing to reduce the inability of cultures and religions to speak to each other. Our survival may well depend on whether everyone, religious or not, can cultivate a certain appreciation for the religion of others, to arrive at a fair and nuanced assessment of it. Both sides have to be seen: religion is a vital force that can find expression in fanaticism, but it also embodies the promise that the energy of evil can be transformed into blessing.

For this task, the Bible is an excellent textbook. In it we find ideologies of conquest and calls for genocide (today euphemized as "ethnic cleansing"). In it we also find love of neighbors extended to include strangers. We find the holy and the unholy side by side. From it one can learn the religious language of myth and legend, ritual and ethos. Only someone who has gained an appreciation of one of the many religious languages can understand the others—just as a mother tongue gives access to other languages. Without empathy for religious thought and behavior, the world would lose a language that we have discovered as a common bond at the very moment when we face a worldwide crisis.

The Bible gives access to a widely used symbolic language. It is unnecessary to grasp at theories of archetypal structures within the collective unconscious that are reflected in universal symbols. It is enough to assume that all great religions are reflexes of primary religions, such as we encounter in tribal religions of Africa, preserved only by oral traditions. Here we find basic prototypes of ritual, myth, and ethos. The secondary scriptural religions incorporate them in modified form. That is why we constantly find analogies and parallels in different religions. They go back to common roots in tribal religions. But their subsequent development also displays a certain common typology. Only this can account for our observation that monasticism does not appear in just one scriptural religion, mysticism in another, sacred scriptures in a third, and so on. Only this can explain how Christian missions found a parallel in the missions of Asiatic religions. Appreciation of the language of primary religious forms and its subsequent development in secondary scriptural religions ("world religions") is today a goal of general educational formation, insofar as it really seeks to address "central problems" of the present.

The Bible's Contribution to Individual Identity

Even when the religion of the Bible is not part of a person's own identity, debate with it can help clarify one's own self-conception. It becomes a catalyst of one's own life-altering decisions. Today there are three possible responses to it, each comprising a broad spectrum of variations:

1. *Critical dismissal* is one common response. In extreme cases, the Bible and Christianity can embody a person's negative identity, that is, what he or she wants *not* to be, from which he or she has been freed or emancipated. The Bible then assists a secular self-conception through dissociation. Even in this case, it is an element of general culture. Today those who reject God mean the God of the Bible.
2. Less common is *deliberate selective reception*, which accepts certain features and rejects others, without feeling at home in the religion of the Bible. And yet the Bible still exerts its influence, if only as a heritage to be preserved. It would be wrong to discredit this selective recourse to religious traditions as patchwork religion. Behind it stands an intuition that choices based on critical distinctions are necessary.
3. *Positive affirmation* can be anything from liberal hermeneutical appropriation to fundamentalist defiance. Even here the continuance of the biblical tradition is always selective. This selection from the Bible's content is usually made unconsciously; consciously, the individual often intends to continue the biblical tradition in its fullness.

For each of these three possibilities, we can sketch many variants in our efforts to achieve clarity about the range of life's possibilities and decisions. Reduction to the either/or of belief or unbelief does not do justice to life. Both belief and unbelief can appeal to the Bible in many different ways. And there are positions that are neither firm belief nor firm unbelief. But objective knowledge of the faith embodied in the Bible is equally important for all positions. An open approach to the

Bible must be pluralistic and expect many different attitudes on the part of those it addresses.

Here we come to the central problem of such an open approach, addressed not just to believers but to all. Is it possible to understand the Bible in its very core from without—as a religious document that seeks to open a dialogue with God? Can this relationship to transcendence be communicated to those who personally want nothing to do with it? Is it possible to interpret this dimension of the Bible without turning it into an existential appeal that improperly puts pressure on those addressed? Is it true, as the Swiss theologian Ingolf Dalferth once avered, that with God there are no bystanders? I would like to take the position that understanding the religious dimension of biblical texts is important for all—for atheists, so that they may better understand the religious self-conception of others, and for Christians, so that they may better understand themselves. Why should those who are religious and those who are not have no language to speak about religious questions? In a pluralistic society, it is possible to discuss them without a sense of missionary coercion or confessional pressure. Pluralism and toleration may present many irritations in our postmodern culture, but on this point they bring progress that can fundamentally alter how we understand and approach the Bible.

An Outsider's View:
The Findings of an Imagined Study of Religion

To help us picture such an understanding of religion from without, I will present a thought experiment with a touch of science fiction. Let us imagine that there are intelligent beings on another planet whose technology is so advanced that they can acquire and assess information about people on Earth. Their worldview is scientific. They do not know what religion and belief are, thus they are all the more eager to find out what people do when they act religiously—when they go to church, pray, observe rituals that accompany life from the cradle to the grave, and read the Bible. What do Earthlings do when they believe in God or doubt God's existence? When they listen to prophets and revelators and consider certain commandments sacred and inviolable? To study these questions, these intelligent beings establish an institute for the interplanetary study of religion. The following presents their findings in a language that draws on images, analogies, and fables from the natural world.

The first finding: People live in a finite and limited world that is not identical with reality per se. Their world conforms to the specific possibilities of the human body, its senses and its cerebrum. Human senses perceive only a portion of the spectrum: they do not perceive ultraviolet and infrared radiation as light. If people had different sensory organs, this radiation would be perceived as visible light. Interestingly, they suspect and know that the world in which they live is not identical with reality per se. They know that reality is greater than the portion of it they perceive, reconstruct, and interpret. They articulate this knowledge that their own world is limited in philosophy and religion. Some of them use the fable of the two frogs to illustrate the situation:

> Once there was a frog that lived at the bottom of a pit. The walls were so tall and steep that he never had a chance to get out. He had never seen the world outside the pit. For him there were only puddles on the bottom of the pit, some mud, and a few stunted plants. Then another frog tumbled into the little world of the pit from the outside world and told of enormous meadows, huge lakes, murmuring reeds. The first frog asked, "How big is an enormous meadow?" And he jumped from the edge of the pit into the middle and asked, "As big as that, or even bigger?" But the frog from the outside world shook his head and said, "They are much bigger." "No," said the first frog, "that's impossible." And jumping from one edge of the pit to the other he asked, "Are these meadows as big as that?" And again the other frog shook his head and said, "They are much bigger, unimaginably big." Then the first frog became angry and shouted, "You're a liar! Get out! You're out of your mind! You're crazy!"

What is the difference between a frog in a pit and a human being? Human beings can conceive that beyond the familiar world in which they live there is a world that is infinitely greater, more complex, and more mysterious. They can realize that the pit in which they live is a construct of the brain, which processes what their senses tell them of the world in a certain way. But they also have a need to relate to reality as a whole—including the reality that is out of reach and inaccessible. And to that end they develop religion, as a culture that can relate to what is inaccessible, what is beyond their knowledge, what sets limits to their will, to which they cannot respond appropriately with their emotions.

The second finding of our interplanetary students of religion: The limits of the human world are not absolute. Some people have experiences that transcend their world. They are like the visionary frog that fell into the pit and gave his companion an inkling of the larger reality. When in the course of human history something of reality per se breaks through, they call that revelation. Humans find such revelations in the great founders of the world's religions, who can be compared to frogs that fell into a pit and were dismissed by other frogs as lunatics and liars. But how is that conceivable? Our scholars have developed a theory: every organ is a structure that helps humans adapt to the world around them. The same is true of beliefs, codes of conduct, and symbols—they are all human attempts to adapt ideas and behavior to the world around them, so that they contain "advance information" about that world. Now we know that organs can change through mutation, so that (in rare cases) their adaptive value increases. They make the world about humans more accessible than it had been. At some point in time, mutations changed the gills of fish into lungs—and as a result the world of dry land was opened to living creatures. Similarly, changes in beliefs, behaviors, and emotional models open new realms of reality. The individuals in whom such changes take place are experienced as revelators by the world around them. Here, too, a frog fable will illustrate the point—the fable of the fish and the tadpole:

A fish and a tadpole were in love. When the tadpole turned into a frog, he jumped onto the dry land. He was able to breathe as a frog and discovered the enormous world beyond the pool where they had grown up. He jumped back into the pool and raved to his friend the fish about the wonderful world. But the fish sighed, "I can't follow you there. Without water I shall die." The frog said, "If you really love me, you will go wherever I go. So do you really love me or not?" The fish whispered, "I love you." "Well then," rasped the frog, "come along." And the fish jumped out onto the dry land and died of love.

This fable tells us that humans are like tadpoles. Some develop into frogs, undergo a transformation, and thus have access to new worlds. The others follow after them—sometimes simply because they "love" some of their more advanced fellows. The great revelators in the history of religion are like tadpoles that developed into frogs with above-average speed—and are followed by others, who are often overtaxed.

The third finding of our scholars: Human beings do not simply experience total reality as a mysterious world into which they grow. This total reality brought them forth. They are creatures of the total system of all things. Ultimately everything that exists—every cell, every nerve, every organ, every idea—was created by this total reality and exists only because it accords with the total system of reality. For all life senses a harsh pressure to adapt. Reality does not accommodate all the various forms of life that arise through an endless process of trial and error or mutation and selection. It "selects" a few that are "better adapted" than the others—that is, who are more competent to survive and multiply in the competition to live. This harsh selective pressure shapes not only the biological basis of life but also the world humans live in as a whole—including its social institutions and philosophical convictions, its science and its religion. In science this selective pressure manifests itself as a severe rigor against which hypotheses and theories are dashed. Where scientific standards are maintained, especially those of the natural sciences, humans are constantly sacrificing their hypotheses and theories on the "altar of reality." In short, all life—from the protozoon to the cerebrum, from the behavior of the ant to the hypotheses of a Nobel laureate—is subject to a draconian selective pressure.

In religious consciousness, this universal dependence on the total system of reality manifests itself as a sense of "creatureliness," of dependence on God, an ultimate reality that determines everything that is. The human relationship to this total reality is ambivalent. On the one hand, human beings rejoice in their existence, their bodies, their senses, which they experience as felicitous and appropriate. They praise God for their existence and for life in general. It is as though life is engaged in a great dialogue with itself and religion is the growing awareness of and participation in this dialogue. Gratitude marks its beginning. But there is another side. Total reality has done more than bring humans forth as felicitous living beings: it also exercises control over everything that takes place. It is not permissive: many things break down and fail because humans do not conform to this total reality. Above all, though, this life is transitory. Its certain end is death. Only death makes possible the fresh variations on life that emerge with each new generation. Only death enables natural selection and hence evolution of life. But all this is bound up with infinite pain. Besides gratitude for their dependence on the total system of reality, humans also feel dread of its selective pressure. In their primitive religious imagination, this includes dread of the Last Judgment, which says: from the variations on life and behavior, ultimate reality—that is, God—selects those that are successful, adapted to the larger world beyond the one humans know, within which this limited world is only a tiny island. Again, we may use the image of tadpoles and frogs to illustrate:

> In the beginning, tadpoles and small fish lived side by side in the pond. They could hardly be distinguished from each other. But when it came down to sallying forth onto dry land, entering a new world, then there had to be a distinction. Only those that had developed lungs could live on land. The others had to stay in the water. A separation ensued. A "judgment" was carried out.

What is the difference between tadpoles, frogs, fish, and the human world? Human beings are all alike. Among humans there are no fundamental insuperable differences like the difference between fish and frogs. Human beings differ not in their biological organs but in their behavior, their dispositions—everything for which they can be responsible. And therefore they dread failure to make the most of life, living their lives regardless of the total reality of all things and failing through their own fault. They do not simply live out their lives: they lead their lives and know that they can fail. They also suspect that they might lead a life that could be repudiated by the total system of reality because it is based on an illusion.

And now we come to a fourth finding of our scholars: Religions embody an antiselectionist protest. From their distant vantage point, our scholars have observed and compared the religions of humankind. They have discovered common features among them—above all, common ways of dealing with ambivalence toward the total system of reality: gratitude for the success of life and dread of its failure. But everywhere—and clearly in the religion of the Bible—they find a feature that would nullify this dread of failure. For here there is a promise that transforms the selective pressure of reality into unconditional acceptance. Here there arises a trust that ultimate reality does not simply screen humanity to identify fit and unfit variations of life, but also accepts the unfit variations—without preconditions. The only "condition" is faith in this message and trust that in the end ultimate reality does not repudiate any form of life, that all will be preserved, that nothing will be lost, even if humans do not know how that happens. This assurance is communicated by one of those figures who is like the visionary frog that fell into a pit. Such a "messenger from above" brought the message that all human beings are destined to outgrow the limited world in which they live. As long as they remain within their limited world and think in its categories, they are forced to judge and condemn all other human beings as fit or unfit, good or bad, competent or incompetent. For human beings this is as obvious as water for a fish. But the tadpole that has become a frog knows that life is also possible in another medium, in air. The world of draconian selection based on the criterion "fit or unfit," "competent or incompetent," is not the whole of reality. The crucial message from that larger and more inclusive world is that there every individual is acknowledged unconditionally—without regard to person, gender, race, origin; regardless of his or her works and competence. In the world of our experience, this unconditional recognition can be compared only to what human beings experience as love—a sense of simple acceptance. The message that communicates this unconditional acknowledgment, that nullifies the pressure of natural selection, is the gospel, to which the Bible bears witness. But this antiselectionist protest also speaks in nonbiblical religions, especially in Buddhism, which withdraws from the agonizing process of mutual competition and replacement.

A fifth finding is also important for us: Religions surround their foundations, founders, scriptures, and teachings with an aura of holiness. Antiselectionist insights themselves, which run counter to life, threaten to fall victim to the principle of natural selection if they are not protected against being forgotten and repressed. They are in danger of extinction because they contravene elemental necessities of life. They are therefore absolutized as the incursion of an alternate reality. The founding figures are made unassailable, the documents that bear witness to them are exempted from criticism, basic insights are turned into dogma. The Christian religion uses all three strategies to defend against oblivion. It has wrapped its founder in the radiance of divinity, enshrined the documents that bear witness to him in a Bible, formulated basic truths as an unassailable creed—while simultaneously, contrary to its intention, opening the door to criticism, because the revealed, written, and proclaimed forms of the "Word of God" mutually relativize themselves. Beyond doubt, however, of these three forms it is the person of Jesus that Christianity most absolutizes: he is preexistent and uncreated. By contrast, Islam instead absolutizes the Qur'an received from Muhammad, viewing it as uncreated and eternal. Yet Muslims can assess the traditions concerning the life of Muhammad (the so-called Hadith) critically and reject many of them as implausible. Buddhism, finally, absolutizes the teaching of the Buddha—and can therefore relativize all other sources of authority. It is unimportant whether the Buddha actually lived. It is unimportant whether the sacred scriptures of Buddhism contain his authentic word. The truth of the teaching ascribed to him rests on itself. An aura is always imposed that exempts certain figures and entities from relativization in order to make them resistant to erosion.

According to this briefly outlined view, religion is a world of conviction and belief that has adapted to objective reality through a long evolutionary process of trial and error, coming to increasingly paradoxical "findings" that it seeks to protect against erosion and relativization. As we shall see later, what shapes religion is not just the external pressure to adapt but also an internal program, just as the development of all organisms is dependent on their internal potential. For now, however, our imaginary account of an interplanetary study of religion—viewing it from without—can illustrate the possibility of interpreting religious experience to outsiders, so that they may see it as something more than a pathologically distorted perception of reality. It is possible to develop an understanding of religion without turning from an observer into a convert.

AN INSIDER'S VIEW: THE INDISPENSABILITY OF RELIGION

We have chosen a fictional view from without to ask whether it is possible to understand religion. It is equally important to ask whether the observers will have questions that open them to a religious interpretation of life. So let us return to Earth in our thought experiment and ask, What would we lose if we ignored the question of God?

1. There would be no communication about the *meaning* of life and the world. Everything that is meaningful becomes meaningful through integration into a larger context, and a partial meaning inevitably implies the question of a larger meaning; therefore, the question of the meaning of the whole leads nowhere. Of course, there are particular events that we spontaneously experience as meaningful, such as the birth of a child or human willingness to help. But we also have meaningless experiences that make no sense at all. Therefore, it seems plausible to posit: either there is a comprehensive meaning, created by a comprehensive meaning-giver, or there is none. What would be the function of the Bible here? Through the Bible we can make contact with this comprehensive giver of meaning! Of course, another position is also defensible: our situation in the world may demand an ungroundable decision to take our cue more from meaningful events than from events that are meaningless. That would also be an act of faith. In the Bible we would have a book that encourages us to defy meaninglessness.

2. There would be no awareness of something in which we can believe with our whole *heart*. In his interpretation of the First Commandment, Martin Luther defines the concept of God: "To have a God is nothing else than to trust and believe him from the whole heart." The question of God thus asks, What can I believe in with my whole heart? In what can I trust? What ultimately matters to me? With religion comes a sense of the absolute, of something that engages us absolutely, a source of stability. What would the function of the Bible be here? It bears witness to an absolute demand—and a warning against absolutizing anything contingent. That, in the Bible, is idolatry. It reveals our tendency to believe with our whole heart in something finite and warns us not to be misled.

3. There would be no ethical orientation to give life its *proper measure*. An appeal to religion will not provide unassailable ethical norms, but it is possible to agree that our norms and values do not depend solely on positive laws and human conventions. States, laws, and customs are not the final court of appeal. Furthermore, ethical consensus is far more difficult for positive norms than for boundaries that must not be transgressed. Finally, "rational" creation of a new ethos is

impossible, but not rational scrutiny of an existing ethos. What would be the function of the Bible here? For the limits of any ethos it teaches a great lesson: the commandment of God differs from human commandments. It is a given. We find it awkwardly presented in tradition. Scrutiny of that tradition is up to us. Above all, however, it teaches us how to deal with the limits of an ethos: we shall never be able to fulfill all ethical norms perfectly.

4. There would be no knowledge of what is *beyond our reach*. Here we see that we have much more control over negative aspects of life than over positive aspects. I can end my life, but I cannot create it. Beyond our reach are both the preconditions for our actions (the laws of nature, our roots and history, where we live) as well as the limits of our actions. Often we are not cognizant of the preconditions. They are too obvious for us to be conscious of them. And we are excruciatingly conscious of the limits. Religion includes a sense that would otherwise atrophy for what is beyond our reach. Here, too, the Bible bears admirable witness.

In conclusion: This question of a religious dimension of reality need not find expression in traditional notions of God. But a sensibility for this religious dimension opens people to the Bible and can be learned in dealing with the Bible. Of course, self-reflection can open people to many things. But they often need external stimuli to uncover what has been buried. The Bible can be such a stimulus.

One task of an open approach to the Bible, therefore, is to make the Bible accessible to all as a language of religious experience. Such a reading of the Bible is one element of a general education. Many will wonder whether the last few paragraphs do not take us beyond *general* education and into the realm of *religious* education. Has the Bible here turned into a document of religious commitment instead of a cultural document? In response we say: understanding the conditions that make religion possible is important, even for someone who has no ear for "religions." A sense for this possibility of human self-conception, realized in many forms upon this earth, should be part of any curious person interested in human life in all its fullness. Understanding a religious language is not the same thing as using it. Only acquisition and use of religious language turns religious experiences into experiences of the divine.

But the interpretation of biblical texts as possible experiences of transcendence is not the only goal of studying the Bible. It has other goals as well. They are reflected in the goals of religious education, which assigns the Bible a variety of roles. It is worth examining these goals more closely.

CHAPTER 2

Biblical "Essentials"

College students aren't the only people who know there is never enough time to read all one would like to read. It is impossible to study, let alone "cover," everything one would like to learn. That's why teachers like me want to search out the most important points about a subject. Those teachers who assign the Bible only a marginal role in their courses necessarily have to ask, What should I teach in the time available? Those who devote more extensive attention to the Bible must say what they find in the Bible that is important enough to justify this extra attention. But nothing in the world is a self-explicating object of study. The key to effective teaching is knowing how to make the subject *accessible* to people encountering it for the first time, and what in the subject is most engaging to the learner. That is no less true for the Bible.

How should we go about deciding what in the Bible is *essential?*

From the standpoint of a teacher, that question means finding what is accessible and engaging in the Bible: What is fundamental in the basic structures of biblical texts? What in them is elemental for life and for learning? What in them is exemplary of the whole? If we can answer those questions, we can approach the Bible with some hope of gaining not just random knowledge of this and that but familiarity with its fundamental structures.

But I want to go further and ask, How does whatever we learn bring us into dialogue with other people? The ability to engage in real dialogue is important for our historical situation, in which people with differing convictions must find common ground. These questions—What is fundamental in the material? What is elemental in its applicability to human life? What is exemplary for study? What supports real communication and dialogue?—are the subject of this chapter.

What Are the "Elementals" in the Bible?

What are the fundamental, elemental structures in the Bible? We are looking here for core biblical beliefs and primary motifs. These will allow us to present an overall description of the biblical viewpoint—what in some circles might be called a biblical theology—that draws on the deep structures of the Bible's textual world without having to set forth its wealth of detail. We then can go on to ask what it is in these fundamental motifs that can shape people's lives. *Textual motifs* thus become *existential motifs.* We can regard as the essential core of the Bible those elements that enrich our fundamental experiences of life and make possible an "identification" with the Bible that can transcend the vicissitudes of biography and history.

We are also looking for those aspects of the Bible that promote dialogue in a pluralistic society. Any understanding of the Bible has to prove its worth in three dialogues: dialogue with secular society, with other religions, and among different Christian denominations. Such dialogues do not end up with simply affirming one's own traditions, of course. Today we affirm our own traditions only in dialogue with others. None of us can possess a genuinely Jewish or Christian identity, for example, if we are unable to present it to others in the hope that they will understand and respect us in our foundational beliefs.

The Bible's Basic Thought Structure

Asking about the "elementals" in the Bible means trying to simplify without neglecting anything essential. Simplification occurs when science reduces processes to rules, variety to types, particulars to generalities. Of course, reality is always more complex than our representations of it, but it is better to have some sort of order within our heads (even if it "simplifies" reality) than to be completely confounded by the sheer complexity of things.

In biblical scholarship, it has usually been the task of so-called biblical theology to summarize the fundamental content of the Bible. In the twentieth century, one of the most influential approaches was the existentialist interpretation of Rudolf Bultmann. This approach identifies a core in the New Testament: the proclamation of the cross and resurrection of Jesus, which transforms believers through faith as they die and rise with Christ. Life before and after this transformation is interpreted in existentialist categories of authentic and inauthentic existence. The difference between the old life and the new is that prior to faith, individuals sought to realize their authentic life by their own efforts, whereas in faith they receive it as a gift. This interpretation of the New Testament message is Protestant to the core. At its center stands the promise of true life *sola gratia* (by grace alone), *sola fide* (by faith alone), without any demands of the law; the law leads people astray. On this view, the Bible is in essence *kerygma*—proclamation—an invitation to decision, in which the fact of salvation trumps any ethical imperative that flows from it. Here the fundamental core of the Bible consists in the basic structures of human existence, which happen to have found expression in biblical texts. But Bultmann's blueprint is insufficiently nuanced, not least with regard to categories of existence. It is dominated by interpretive categories like fear, anxiety, and death, authenticity and inauthenticity. These are in keeping with the anthropology of existential philosophy, but not with the totality of life reflected in the Bible. Where, for example, are joy, praise, and thanksgiving, as encountered in the Psalms? Where are aggression and reconciliation, which inform the Joseph novella? Where are justice and prophetic criticism? Where are obligation and relief from burdens through the institutions of the law codes of the Old Testament? The existential approach is one-sidedly "existentialistic," that is, individualistic.

The salvation-history theology of Oscar Cullmann offered a real alternative. Here the crucial point is not the transformation of individuals, but changes over the course of history. God's historical involvement with humanity begins universally with everyone and looks toward a universal end. Between the beginning and end, because of human failure, God pursues the divine purpose with representative groups: because of universal sin, God chooses Israel to represent humankind; because of Israel's sin, God chooses a remnant; because of the failure of the remnant, at last God chooses a single individual, Jesus of Nazareth, who in turn chooses the twelve apostles as a new "remnant," reflecting symmetrically the previous course of history. These apostles found the church, which corresponds to Israel. But the church lives vicariously on behalf of all, to bring them to God through its missionary message. On this view, the Bible is essentially an interpretation of history. It does not confront the world with the need for a decision but tells of events into which people can integrate themselves. The fundamental core of the Bible consists in the basic structures of history: universality, particularity, and successive vicarious representation in a more and more restricted group. These constitute the categories of this biblical blueprint of history. This salvation-history approach stood in the shadow of existential interpretation, but its focus on humanity as a whole gives it a cast every bit as modern as existential interpretation with its focus on the individual.

In this book I rely on a third scheme, an interpretation of biblical religion based on the theory of religions. According to this theory, as widely taught in religious studies courses in colleges and universities, religions are historical symbol-systems, structures made up of symbols, constructed by human beings in order to worship God. We recognize their distinctiveness in basic recurring rules, the principles by which the "cathedrals" of meaning in each religion are under constant construction. On this view, the fundamental core of the Bible thus comprises basic structures of religious language: its grammar, so to speak, but a grammar that regulates not just texts but also rituals and ethics. This grammar is learned (usually unconsciously) in the context of religious socialization; further education brings it to consciousness.

These three schemes operate with modern interpretive categories. If we finally turn to the Bible and ask which scheme is most typically represented in the biblical writings themselves, of course there can be only one answer: what is fundamental is its God. Everything else serves to give access to this God. God is accessible through God's "Spirit." Using the ancient principle that like is known by like, the Apostle Paul declares: "For what human being knows what is truly human except the human spirit that is within? So also no one comprehends what is truly God's except the Spirit of God" (1 Cor. 2:11). This Spirit is linked to the Word (meaning the Bible); it does not disclose itself through the written letter but through the living Word, for "the letter kills, but the Spirit gives life" (2 Cor. 3:6). The Spirit writes God's will on the hearts of humans (2 Cor. 3:6), moving them to understand and do God's will from within. Christ gives this freedom: "The Lord is the Spirit, and where the Spirit of the Lord is, there is freedom" (2 Cor. 3:17). The sense of the Bible is therefore that the Spirit opens human beings to the fundamental core of the Bible—that is, to God—and opens the text of the Bible to human beings, so that they can accept it. Without the Spirit, a veil lies over Scripture, frustrating its true understanding (2 Cor. 3:14). In this viewpoint, which arises from the Bible itself, texts, narratives, and images are fundamental only insofar as they contain the "spirit of the Bible" and give access to God. If we know what this biblical "spirit" *is,* we could answer two other crucial questions raised earlier: What in the Bible enables Jewish and Christian identity? And what enables dialogue between human beings, religions, and denominations? Borrowing from the Bible, we can say: not the Bible's *letter,* but its *spirit* grounds biblical identity through the passing ages. But identity must be presented in dialogue with others if it is not to erode. The place of the Spirit is not just in dialogue within the church; like the wind, it "blows where it chooses" (John 3:8). It brings human beings together even when they speak different languages, as in the miracle of Pentecost (Acts 2:1ff.). In the self-concept of the Bible, then, the question of what is fundamental leads to the question of what promotes dialogue.

A Foundation for Learning and Life

It is one thing, of course, to identify fundamental structures within the Bible, and another to discover that they are simple enough to be immediately accessible to the reader, even without a sophisticated theological background, and that they are elemental enough to human life that they are immediately sensible in extreme situations such as life crises. Given that, the "elementals" of the Bible will include

- *symbols* such as God or Christ, which correspond to the two core beliefs of the earliest Christian religion, monotheism and faith in the Redeemer;
- *traditions*, which we will use to identify the basic motifs of the texts; and
- *relational aspects* of both symbols and traditions, the existential motifs that shape and inform life.

For example, *that God created a trustworthy world, in which life can succeed,* is an elemental datum of faith. Fundamental trust is a basic relational quality. Childhood religious education begins with this trust; adults return to it in times of crisis. This trust undergoes development until adulthood is reached. This trust is associated with central *symbols:* God is creator, shepherd, rock. God takes us by the hand and guides us through life. We find such images in a few important *traditions,* as in Psalm 23, "The Lord is my shepherd," and the words of trust in Psalm 73, "Nevertheless I am continually with you; you hold my right hand. You guide me with your counsel, and afterward you will receive me with honor. Whom have I in heaven but you? And there is nothing on earth that I desire other than you" (vv.23-25). Just as elemental are narrative texts like the story of Noah and the flood, at the end of which God promises: "As long as the earth endures, seedtime and harvest, cold and heat, summer and winter, day and night, shall not cease" (Gen. 8:22). Anyone who has grown up with the language of the Bible will remember internalizing these words as a defense against childish fears. They still echo in adulthood: the rainbow against the dark clouds is a sign that God will keep God's word, regardless!

That such fundamental trust surfaces repeatedly in crises is a universal experience. That is why Erik Erikson's theory of the human life cycle has proved so popular. According to Erikson, people must constantly strive to balance opposing tendencies: in childhood, trust versus mistrust, autonomy versus shame and doubt, initiative versus guilt; in latency and adolescence, industry versus inferiority, identity versus role confusion; in adulthood, intimacy versus isolation, generativity versus stagnation; and finally, ego integrity versus despair in old age. Without necessarily buying into the sequence of phases or their psychoanalytic foundation, we can recognize here universal conflicts that religious symbols address. It is also clear that this theory not only interprets empirical observation but also sets goals. It is not just that life involves reconciliation of opposing tendencies: it is *meant* to be so.

Basic Structures and Contents of the Bible
We could discuss at length whether there are facts and situations that are universally exemplary. My interest is narrower, however. Since in fact people even in a secular society make routine appeal to the exemplary quality of one or another biblical character or story, I want to ask: Which biblical texts and themes have exemplary value for as many other people as possible?

Biblical texts are of various sorts. Treatment of one sort of text provides practice in dealing with all texts of the same sort. Narrative, poetic, legal, and argumentative texts of the Bible can therefore be treated as exemplary, as well as the various biblical genres identified by that area of biblical scholarship called form criticism. In principle no single sort of text is privileged. Central themes appear in all the forms: creation is recorded as *narrative*; trust is expressed in *prayer* (Psalm 23); monotheism is mandated in a *commandment* (Exod. 20:2); justification is expounded in a *disputatious letter* (Romans); theodicy—the question of God's justice—is examined in *wisdom dialogue* (Job). The Bible is not a homogeneous text but a compendium of different forms and genres. Each must be appreciated on its own terms. Form criticism is unquestionably helpful in the search for exemplary texts.

In addition, the Bible is a collection of many books, each with its own rhetorical agenda, which redaction criticism—the method that examines how the Gospel-writers edited the material available to them—has identified. Mark's Gospel is a call to discipleship. Matthew demands a "better righteousness," summarized in the Sermon on the Mount. Luke's two books are a call to repentance: all its major figures, from the Baptist through Jesus to Peter and Paul, are preachers of repentance. The three parables of loss and repentance constitute the internal center of the Gospel of Luke (Luke 15).

Finally, historical epochs are apparent in the Bible. The reader may follow the course of history presented in the Bible from the time of the patriarchs to the dawn of Christianity. It is a more complex matter, of course, to adopt one of the many scholarly reconstructions of different moments in its literary and religious history and to regard it as exemplary: for example, does one privilege an initial phase in Israel of intolerant prophetic debate when a small, "Yahweh-alone" minority stood in opposition to the majority, or the second, subsequent phase of more tolerant debate, recorded in the Pentateuch, in which conflicting theologies stood side by side, or a third phase in the postexilic period, when Israel entered upon the stage of international debate in wisdom writings like Job and novellas like Jonah? What is *typical* of an epoch is another potential criterion for selecting exemplary texts and problems.

Identifying fundamental motifs and themes provides yet another principle of selection, which can also be applied to those already mentioned. If we can succeed in identifying essential fundamental features of the world of the biblical text, then just one exemplar of each suffices to illustrate the motifs of creation, wisdom, the exodus, and so forth—although two would be better, so that comparison can show how the same motif recurs with variations. The creation motif, for example, finds expression in many different texts and forms: as *mythological narrative* in Genesis 1–2, as a *hymn* in the prologue to John, as a *disputatious argument* in Romans 1:18-32.

What Is "Dialogical" in the Bible?

In a modern pluralistic society, of course, people are separated not just through their vocations but also through their political, religious, and cultural roots. In this situation, it is important to ask what forms of Bible study help or hinder social cohesion. I'm particularly interested, then, to ask to what extent the religion of the Bible can foster dialogue, not least because there is a general doubt in contemporary Western culture as to whether the Bible can enter into dialogue at all with the secular world and with other religions. My question is: What is there in the Bible that can connect us with other human beings? What can help us to promote dialogue with them? And what in the Bible can stand in the way?

Dialogue always proceeds on two levels. On the objective level, the participants exchange points of view; and in this sense, dialogues may resemble arguments. At the same time, though, on the relational level participants exchange deference and esteem. They may experience themselves as relatively distant or relatively close. When participants are distant, we take the possibility of misunderstanding as a given and are happy whenever we find agreement; the very existence of dialogue is a plus. When the participants are closer, on the other hand, we take consensus as a given and are therefore all the more taken aback by misunderstandings. The objective level and the relational level are always present, but one can be more or less dominant. Relational problems also intrude in discourses that pursue arguments.

Dialogue with the Secular World
On the surface, dialogue with secularity is often predominantly argumentative. It enshrines a great tradition of religious interpretation and religious criticism. Here we may draw on a complex and sophisticated body of thought, such as that of Karl Marx, Friedrich Nietzsche, and Sigmund Freud, who presented astute arguments regarding the Bible. These great critics of religion are among the fathers of the modern world who contributed to the notion that this world has been emancipated

by protest against religion and the Bible. The emotional aura of this emancipation sometimes is disruptive on the relational level. Both sides exchange philosophical arguments about religion, but we are each really struggling for respect. In dialogue with secularity, the participants are often unconscious of the relational level, but it would be better for them to be conscious of it.

Interreligious Dialogue

Interreligious dialogue, by contrast, begins with expectations of substantial empathy. It often embodies a mystical piety that would like to use the similarity of religious experience to circumvent the differences between religions. Mysticism appears to be the same throughout all religions. Nevertheless, we repeatedly enter into this conversation with false expectations. We must enter alien worlds gradually, since immediate empathy is not possible. Only by this laborious process does interfaith dialogue slowly become argumentative discourse. Interfaith dialogue must always strive to transcend expressions of good will and achieve discursive clarity.

Interconfessional Dialogue

Ecumenical dialogue—that is, between different groups of Christians— often takes as given a closeness that is simply not present. Official discussion of the interchange between doctrinal positions is left to the handful of ecumenical "pros." The majority feels it more important that the dialogue should affirm an already existing commonality, rather than to explore differences. Dialogue plays a communicative role among participants who have a sense of togetherness, who not only speak with each other but live and celebrate together.

The task facing every dialogue is to achieve a balance between the objective level and the relational level. Often when the participants believe they are already well on their way on the relational level, further discussion brings out differences. On the other hand, when discussion is astonishingly intellectual, the relational level must be kept in view.

Emphasizing what is elemental and what is dialogical in the biblical tradition requires this balance. Even when defining what is elemental in the Bible, there is always a struggle for the potential respect of others!

CHAPTER 3

The Heart of the Bible:
Core Themes

The "spirit of the Bible" can be expressed not only in theological terms but also in the categories of religious studies. Like all religions, the Christian religion is a symbolic language. It consists of *stories* and linguistic *images,* as well as *rituals* such as baptism and the Lord's Supper, and *material objects* such as cross and book, altar and church. Protestantism legitimizes all forms of religious symbolism by the criterion of the Bible. What cannot be justified from the biblical text (for instance, the indisputable authority of an infallible church) is not recognized. All these religious tokens and symbols taken together constitute a kind of "language" with which human beings make contact with God.

How do we know that religion constitutes a language, a coherent whole? Every language (including the symbolic languages of different religions and denominations) is governed by *rules.* In such natural languages as English, German, and French, these are grammatical rules—rules that determine how words are modified and combined; in the symbolic language of religious, they are religious rules. These rules determine which symbols belong to the symbol inventory of a religion and how they can be modified and combined. Conversion, for example, can be described in many ways: conversion to Christianity, a new vocation, illumination through knowledge, remorse for a transgression, or rebirth of the whole person. It can be associated with various (ritual) symbols: baptism, imposition of hands, a prayer, or a fish symbol on a car. But it can never be associated in a positive sense with "sin," since it implies rejection of sin. This was the consensus of the early church. What was disputed was only whether conversion must also bear the mark of "uniqueness" (as in Hebrews, which rejects a second repentance and conversion), or whether an individual can repent and be converted many times, as most churches teach.

We learn the symbolic language of religion as we learn a natural language, without mastering all its rules. We internalize it when we hear the stories of the Bible, celebrate the feasts of the church year, and learn the meaning of the manger and the cross. Just as we unconsciously learn the grammar of our mother tongue by using and hearing it, so we learn the basic rules of the Christian religion by immersion in the symbolic language of religion. And just as only a few grammarians bring the rules of grammar to the level of consciousness, so too in religion: only a relatively few individuals—theologians—are its "grammarians." The fundamental grammatical rules that they teach are the fundamental motifs of the Bible, a few of which have already been introduced: conversion, change of heart, creation, and justification. These motifs are the spirit of the Bible. Whoever comes to believe interprets life and reality in the light of these motifs. They are transmitted historically, bound to the letter—but no more identical with the letter than a grammatical rule is identical with actual sentences formulated with its aid. With the aid of these rules, we repeatedly remake our symbolic religious world and construct "sentences" that may never have been spoken by anyone before and yet belong to the symbolic system of our religion. These rules are the constituent principles of religion. Sometimes as historically transmitted motifs they work hand in hand with human predispositions. Sometimes they stand in tension with human predispositions, such as the bent to hold one's ground at the expense of other living creatures. What is important for us to realize is that the fundamental motifs of faith are learned. They come through "hearing" (see Rom. 10:17: "So faith comes from what is heard, and what is heard comes through the word of Christ"). We internalize them when we hear biblical texts and take them to heart.

Such a "grammatical" approach to the Bible may sound to some readers like a conservative orientation to "what the Bible says," which seeks to create openness to the Word of God as something that comes "from above." But it is also possible to follow this approach within a "liberal" tradition, which interprets religion "from below," for religion is also a human creation. It is a symbolic system, a "semiotic cathedral" built not of stones but of narratives, images, rituals, and objects—in short, symbols of various kinds. Like all churches and cathedrals, it is designed and built by human beings, used and maintained by human beings. But just as it is impossible to understand the Gothic cathedrals if they are not viewed as a hymn of praise to God in stone, so it is impossible to understand the semiotic cathedral of religion if it is not grasped as thanksgiving for the sudden inbreaking of a transcendental reality. Secularized visitors can view it as expressing power and domination as well as human fears and longings. But its significance would escape them if they did not also understand it as a witness to a longing for something "totally other." Some will enter the cathedral to be in the grip of this longing. Others will take aesthetic pleasure in its architecture. Like any structure, this semiotic cathedral has its architectural principles. In religion, these are a few core beliefs and fundamental principles. A first section will outline these fundamental biblical "architectural principles" as a brief summary of the "spirit of the Bible." Subsequent sections will suggest briefly how they can have "elemental" significance in modern life.

THE TWO BASIC BELIEFS OF CHRISTIAN FAITH

The Christian faith rests on two fundamental convictions: monotheism and belief in a Redeemer. The first, belief in the one and only God, it shares with the prophetic religions of Judaism and Islam (and with convergent monotheistic tendencies in ancient "paganism"). The second distinguishes it from those related religions and links it, if only loosely, with the redemption religions of the East—especially if we take into account the role of the Redeemer in the mystical schools of Christianity and primitive Christian Gnosticism. At the center of the Old Testament stands the revelation of the one and only God; at the center of the New Testament stands the Redeemer. The two divisions of the canon correspond to these two fundamental convictions. (I am well aware that Christian students of the Old Testament are often inclined to deny that the Old Testament has its own center, recognizing instead only an "external center" in the New Testament. But this position is defensible only within a Christian interpretation of the Old Testament.)

Monotheism

The first core conviction of the Christian faith is monotheism—belief in the one and only God. Everything in reality, in life and in faith, is related to this ultimate reality and determined by it. This reality is the center of the symbolic language of religion, around which this language is organized, and this reality thus is shown itself to be an independent force distinct from its environment. The effect of this belief is to prohibit other ties: it rules out any association with other gods—and everything that establishes an association with these gods. Nothing may be likened to God. Whatever constitutes the world is not God. Monotheism emerged in the sixth century B.C.E. among two peoples, Jews and Greeks. The biblical prophet known as Deutero-Isaiah and the pre-Socratic philosophers developed an understanding of God that transcended polytheism. Among the pre-Socratics, the idea of monotheism was linked with an attraction to a monistic—that is, unified—explanation of the world. Here, a presumed need of the human mind for interpretations of the world that reduce diversity to unity made itself felt. In this sense, the discovery of logic goes hand in hand with the discovery of the one God. The result was a cognitively motivated monotheism. Israel's monotheism, by contrast, was ethically motivated. Human responsibility is related to a single authority that determines everything in life. God is a brilliant ethical energy that manifests itself as a glowing fire of love, which can blaze into the flames of hell if opposed. In their absolute demands, God's commands enable a unique consistency of conduct. In the conception that each individual is responsible before God for his or her life, a sense of human absoluteness and freedom finds expression.

There is a problem inherent in monotheism: everything that happens in the world, including evil, must be ascribed to the one and only God. Thus, there arises a contradiction between the ethical demands of God and God's own conduct. God cannot be conceived simultaneously as beneficent and omnipotent. We find three ways of dealing with this problem:

1. A first strategy consists in emphasizing God's sovereignty and transcendence. God's thoughts are far removed from human thoughts. God becomes the *deus absconditus*—the hidden God—who must be trusted despite appearances. It is crucial to maintain this relationship of trust through all temptations and ordeals. This is the way of Abraham, who, when commanded to sacrifice Isaac, trusted to the end that God would provide a humane resolution contrary to all appearances. This is the way of Job, who is content to have God communicate with him even though he never gets an answer to his questions about the meaning of his suffering.

2. A second strategy is represented by Job's comforters. They seek to trace human suffering to human guilt. The reader of the Job drama is unquestionably prejudiced against them. But the reader must also admit that such an interpretation has enormous motivating power. An individual who is personally responsible for evil can do something to abolish it, can repent and change. Monotheistic faith is always associated with a heightened sense of guilt. One of its crises comes about when this sense of guilt gains the upper hand.

3. A third strategy basically questions one of the premises of monotheism. As long as people believed in a struggle between various gods, it was easier to interpret the contrariness of the world. If the good is powerless, it is because it is constrained by the power of evil. Within monotheism we find a tendency to ascribe this power of evil, if not to another god, at least to demons and fallen angels. The gulf between God and humanity is peopled with intermediary beings. They exonerate the one and only God from the evil in this world.

Belief in a Redeemer

The second core conviction of Christianity is belief in a Redeemer. It is secondary to the first and stands in some tension with it. It is secondary, because the one and only God is accessible to all peoples only through the Redeemer. Through Christ monotheism becomes universal. The Redeemer serves to affirm belief in the one God and deal with its structural confusions.

1. Belief in the Redeemer reverses the relativization of monotheism through intermediary beings. Christ now becomes Lord of all the demons and angels. He is victorious over all enemies and powers, thus returning sovereignty to God, who at the end will be "all in all" (1 Cor. 15:11-28).

2. Belief in the Redeemer also serves to overcome the heightened human awareness of sins that is structurally associated with monotheism. Its motivating power can easily transform into a paralyzing pessimism. Redemption from sins opens the way to a consistent monotheism.

The desire for absoluteness and responsibility has also shaped this second conviction of the Christian faith: religious reflection furthered the elevation of the historical Jesus to divinity. A contingent figure, constrained by limitations, was interpreted as a manifestation of an eternal, absolute, and commanding being, and was thus surrounded with the mythical aura associated only with a divine being. It is important to note that this figure did not vanish into the aura. Behind the traditions of Jesus, we can still recognize the itinerant Galilean preacher who initially had himself baptized by John and then went his own way with a message of the imminent kingdom of God, successfully addressed it to outsiders, brought on the enmity of the authorities, and was finally executed by the Romans. This memory of Jesus stamped itself indelibly on the traditions. From the start, people related to him as a concrete historical figure, mortal, contingent, and constrained. After his death, however, this earthly figure was integrated into a "high Christology," which, on the basis of the Easter appearances, was seen as more than a human being—the Son of God, who decisively brought about salvation in the history of God and humanity.

People saw in Christ a divine being who came down from heaven to redeem the world: the *Logos* (Word) before all time, who entered into time; the Son of God, far above all humanity, who made himself subject to human contingency; the free figure who was handed over to a world of bondage. This Christology chimes in its inner structure with the human self: a self in which a sense of eternity, absoluteness, and freedom lives—but sees itself irrevocably exposed to the transience, conditions, and constraints of the world. There was truth in the Gnostic vision that interpreted Christ as a symbol of the human self, except theirs was a narcissistic view of the self, as though it were in its innermost core imperishable, unconditional, and unconstrained.

There remains a tension between these two fundamental convictions of the Christian faith. It is resolved with the aid of the first, monotheistic belief: nothing may stand alongside God but God. In lengthy process of reflection, the early church traced the distinction between the Father and the Son to an indivisible unity of being so as to overcome any belief in two or three gods. This relationship is expressed in the doctrine of the Trinity: one substance in three persons (*una substantia, tres personae*). And this same process identified the particular attributes of each "person." God as Creator stands infinitely superior to the divine creation. God is the great mystery of being. God as the Incarnate One identifies Godself unconditionally with human existence. Against the temptation to limit this association to the higher element of humanity or limit it temporally or deny its reality, the notion of the incarnation maintains the uncurtailed identification of God with this one human life. This is the meaning of the two-natures doctrine (Jesus Christ as *vere homo et vere deus*—"truly human and truly God"). God as Holy Spirit continues to identify herself with every human individual. The identification of God with the human individual Jesus was not a one-time event: God's will is to be present in *all the faithful* through the Spirit—not simply to give them assurance of what took place in Jesus, but to renew this event in them as God's presence in their lives.

In my opinion, the doctrine of the Trinity that emerged in early Christianity responds to a fundamental problem in monotheism. If from all the gods only one is left, who is responsible for everything that happens, two insoluble problems arise: the omnipotence of the one and only God is irreconcilable with the suffering of the world if God is also to be considered beneficent. It is also irreconcilable with human freedom, if God determines everything—including human actions. The trinitarian faith gives an answer that is not satisfying theoretically but is livable in practice: in Jesus, God personally takes on the suffering of humanity. God shares the suffering of God's creatures and overcomes their suffering. As Holy Spirit, God gives people freedom and renews their autonomy and dignity. God's omnipotence does not overwhelm human autonomy. Quite the contrary: as the dwelling of the deity, the individual takes on infinite value.

These two fundamental convictions of Christianity early on became criteria for distinguishing true from false Christianity. Alongside the writings of the New Testament canon and local Christian literature consonant with this canon, there were many Gnostic documents that never had a chance to be included in the canon and do not appear as canonical books in any biblical manuscripts. Most of the Gnostic documents were rejected because they teach a subordinate demiurge—an autonomous driving force—who created this imperfect world, while the true God was denied by this very demiurge. The unity of God was a self-evident principle in selecting scriptures and traditions. Ideas that rejected it were discarded. In addition, there was the criterion of belief in the incarnation—not simply an ostensible or transitory conjunction of the divine and human in Christ. Thus, the early church voiced two fundamental decisions: affirmation of the world, which did not originate with a subordinate demiurge but from the beneficent will of the Creator; and affirmation of complete humanity, put on body and soul by God—not partially, temporarily, or ostensibly. The world and humanity were thus sanctified and valorized as the critical locus of salvation, of bane and blessing.

CORE THEMES OF BIBLICAL FAITH

Alongside the two fundamental convictions concerning the one and only God and Jesus the Redeemer, we find in the Bible a "spirit" in which all of life and the world are viewed and interpreted. It comprises many fundamental motifs, beliefs appearing in many books of the Bible, albeit not necessarily in all. It is sufficient that they appear in several books, in conjunction with a variety of themes and genres. They establish a "family likeness" between otherwise disparate documents based on common features. In the following pages I present an open list of such fundamental motifs. The list will never be complete. Neither do the motifs constitute a rigorous system—they are more a loose fabric of rules with points of intersection and contact, like a mobile that is constantly in motion and yet contains a hidden structure. Anyone may try to formulate additional motifs.

Creation
God created the world through the divine will. By God's will, there might have been nothing at all, or everything might have been different. God's creative power is active at every moment; in the midst of history it manifested itself in the resurrection of Jesus from the dead.

The being and nonbeing of all things are ascribed to the one and only God—not to any material distinct from God, not to any demiurge alongside God, not to any emanation from God, but solely to the will of God. There is no other creator, no world, external to God. Fundamentally there is only God and the void—and God's power to create from this void. But it was a long journey from this idea to *creatio ex nihilo*.

Behind the Old Testament creation texts, we can discern three notions of creation: a victorious struggle with chaos (Job 38–41; Isa. 51:9-10); the birth of the world through sexual generation (Gen. 14:19; Isa. 51:1); and the creation of all things by a word of command (Gen. 1:1-31). The third gained general acceptance and at the threshold of the New Testament period led to the first (still formulaic) assertion of *creatio ex nihilo* in 2 Maccabees 7:28: God created out of nothingness. But this nothingness was still a formless "something." Creation is not yet *creatio ex nihilo* in the strict sense (as first conceived by the second-century Gnostic Basilides). But it is creation through the word. Paul speaks of the God "who gives life to the dead and *calls* into existence the things that do not exist" (Rom. 4:17). In the Gospel of John, creation takes place through the "Word," and with this Word a light enters the creation that stands in conflict with the preexisting darkness. The Word brings meaning to creation. It is like a concealed text that humanity can decode. The metaphor of the "book of nature" still draws on this idea of a creation through the Word.

The New Testament presupposes the idea of creation. Nowhere is it developed in detail. We must hear echoes of Old Testament texts when Jesus speaks of the God who causes the sun to rise on the evil and on the good (Matt. 5:45), who feeds the birds of the air and the lilies of the field (Matt. 6:26-30), who counts the hairs of the head and holds every sparrow in the divine hand (Matt. 10:29-31). This belief in creation is omnipresent. God's creative will is present in things great and small: in the origin of the world at the beginning of time (John 1:1-5; 1 Cor. 8:6) and in the arrival of each new day (*1 Clem.* 24:2-3), in the unrepeatable re-creation of an individual as a "new creature" (Gal. 6:5) and in God's ongoing renewal of each new day (2 Cor. 4:16). It is at work in the past event of Jesus' resurrection from the dead and in the future resurrection of all Christians. It fills everything that exists with light and life: "In the beginning was the Word, and the Word was with God, and the Word was God. All things came into being through him, and without him not one thing came into being. In him was life, and the life was the light of all people. The light shines in the darkness, and the darkness did not overcome it" (John 1:1-5). This light shines like the sun behind the clouds, without being seen; only in one place does it break through into the world undisguised, as through a hole in the clouds: in the person of Jesus of Nazareth. "And the Word became flesh and lived among us, and we have seen his glory, the glory as of the Father's only Son, full of grace and truth" (John 1:14).

How can this motif of the Bible become an elemental motif for today? It is the creation motif that allows us to see the world against the background of its possible nonexistence. Nothing is a matter of course, not even mere existence. Every moment is a transition. It emerges for an instant from the "not yet" of the future into the momentary present and vanishes immediately into the "no longer" of the past. In the light of biblical language, God is experienced as the power that accomplishes constant creation from nothing. By understanding the mystery of being as creation, the Bible leads us to transform this challenge into thanksgiving, thanksgiving for each day of life. When amazement at the very existence of the world and the self is transformed into praise and thanksgiving, a supposedly "trivial" circumstance becomes a significant datum of life. Awareness of this transformation makes life more intense. Such a belief in creation is elemental: all human beings—children and adults, students and teachers—can find themselves in it. In the corresponding negative awareness that no one is self-created, an elemental sense of creatureliness survives even the many announcements of the death of God. And in the immediate experience of an all-pervasive contingency, of dependence upon unknown circumstances, it is also immediately real to our secularized contemporaries.

Wisdom

The world was created by God's Word and wisdom (John 1:1-5). This divine wisdom is unattainable through human wisdom, but is still paradoxically accessible through Christ, "in whom are hidden all the treasures of wisdom and knowledge" (Col. 2:3).

An order and rationality that makes life possible determines all things, even if it has more to do with the background than with the foreground of what takes place. Old Testament wisdom assumes that life lived in consonance with the hidden order of God's creation can be successful. Notoriously, this optimism found itself in a crisis: the undeserved suffering of an individual made it impossible to believe that there is an intelligible meaning in all suffering; the meaning of the world (and wisdom) is beyond human understanding (Job 28). And yet this meaning is still clear enough to sharpen our awareness of the world's indifference to the human happiness and suffering and to let us experience absurdity as depressing (Ecclesiastes). The crisis of practical wisdom in the light of God's apparent absence from the order of the world led to a longing for revealed wisdom, made accessible only to a handful of God's elect

(Wisdom of Solomon 6–9; Baruch 3; Sirach 24): this wisdom became personified and autonomous, even though it is fundamentally only an aspect of God, namely God's beneficent side, caring for the world. In the personified figure of Wisdom, the queen of heaven could even resurface as the maternal side of God without endangering monotheism. She was identified with the Torah. In her is revealed the hidden order of the world, which is always less immediately intelligible.

The New Testament does not identify Wisdom with the Torah but with Christ. This identification creates an even greater tension with the world: the messengers of Wisdom are persecuted and killed by those to whom they are sent (Luke 11:49-51). The wisdom of God is hidden from the wise but revealed to the naïve and immature, those who are weary and bearing heavy burdens, although they would otherwise have no access to wisdom (Matt. 11:25-30; 1 Cor. 1:26-27). The gentle wisdom from above is in conflict with aggressive wisdom from below (James 3:13-18). Everywhere wisdom encounters resistance and must assert itself to prevail: cosmically its light encounters the resistance of darkness (John 1:1-5), historically it is rejected in Christ and crucified by the rulers of this world (1 Cor. 2:8), ethically it meets the resistance of the old human nature. Trust in a background order behind the world remains, but the disruption of this order is manifest in the need for God to take the path of foolishness to prevail within the world (1 Cor. 1:18-25): "For God's foolishness is wiser than human wisdom, and God's weakness is stronger than human strength" (1 Cor. 1:25).

The existential significance of the wisdom motif is obvious: it makes people seek a benign hidden order in reality. It is possible simply to take as given the ordered structures of reality, but it is also possible to look on them with amazement and be motivated to look for another structural order—even against all appearances. When we consider that the growth of the natural sciences has increasingly disclosed an order in nature and that an explanation of nature based on a few elementary particles and fundamental forces reveals an overwhelming "rationality," we may see in it the traces of a superior reason of which our own reason is only a pale shadow. That this overwhelming rationality also encourages our own rationality can still be our experience, even after the end of the physico-theological proof of God. The total system of things has given rise to us and developed an intelligence within us that is capable of deciphering the intelligence invested in this system. Of course, all of this can leave someone totally unmoved. But—read in the light of the biblical wisdom motif—it can also be the basis of an elemental affirmation of meaning and a consequent obligation to preserve this meaningful order. This vision can unite us, both old and young: the quest for nature's hidden wisdom still follows the promise that living in consonance with this wisdom is better than living athwart it. But whatever is "wise" in creation can be "foolishness" in the context of particular social circumstances (in the "world").

Miracle

Everything that takes place in the world is open to miraculous events that baffle all expectations. Nothing is totally determined. God and human beings, faith and prayer, effect miraculous changes. Miracles are also signs that point beyond themselves. Jesus is invested with such miraculous power.

A miracle is faith's favorite child. To many, however, it is an illegitimate child, a source of shame. And yet a life-affirming message resides in miracles: nothing is so set in stone that it cannot be altered by miraculous power. The Old Testament bears witness to mighty "signs and wonders" performed by God. God brings his people out of Egypt with mighty acts of power. But human beings as well as God perform miracles in the Old Testament: Moses, Elijah, Elisha.

The New Testament is dominated by such charismatic miracle workers. Jesus and his disciples are engaged in a healing movement. The formula "Your faith has made you well" (Mark 5:34; 10:52; Luke 17:19; and so forth) and the saying about the faith that can move a mountain (Mark 11:22-24; 1 Cor. 13:2) document their conviction that a miraculous power is at work in them through faith and prayer. In the miracle stories, we can sense a vigorous protest against all forms of suffering. It is better to question normal expectations about the course of events than the right of an individual to receive help. Miracles serve almost exclusively to enable and assist life. Punitive miracles are the exception. They are inflicted on people like Ananias and Sapphira, who pretend to provide support but hold back (Acts 5:1-11) or else symbolize a transfer of power, like the withered fig tree (Mark 11:12-14, 20-21). The first Christians possessed extraordinary charismata, such as the "gift of healing" (1 Cor. 12:28). But they also experienced the limits of such power: not all exorcisms were successful (Mark 9:28-29); Paul was not healed of his affliction (2 Cor. 12:9); no miracle saved Jesus from the cross (Mark 15:31-32).

The New Testament also speaks of miracles as signs that interpret events. The star over Bethlehem interprets the birth of Jesus as the appearance of a new ruler (Matt. 2:1-12). An earthquake interprets his death as a cosmic cataclysm (Matt. 27:52); catastrophes signal his return (Matt. 24:4-8). All these are "signs from heaven," such as Jesus himself refused (Mark 8:11-12). Instead he interpreted the miracles taking place on earth as "signs" of the reign of God, pointing to something else still hidden. Thus, Jesus himself is aware of a symbolic interpretation of miracles. When demons are cast out, for him it is a sign of the reign of God and the final victory over evil (Matt. 12:28). In the Synoptic Gospels, individual miracles are symbolically transparent for various meanings: the draft of fishes is a symbol of mission (Luke 5:1-11), the healing of the blind is a symbol of enlightenment (Mark 8:22-25), the storm at sea symbolizes the storms besetting the church (Matt. 8:23-27). A symbolic second meaning shines behind the event itself, without calling it into question. In the Gospel of John, all miracles are fundamentally symbolic, and this symbolic meaning calls into question the obvious immediate meaning. All miracles are images of redemption and revelation: of feeding with heavenly wisdom, of the dawning of the light of faith, of the advent of a new life here and now. Because miracles are understood symbolically, they are associated with highly diverse themes of the New Testament faith. As paradoxical events within the world, they belong to the image of God and Christ, as charismata they belong to its understanding of the church, and as healings they belong to its anthropology. Through miracles the world is drawn into small "enclaves of salvation" in the work of redemption. Merely to apprehend the immediate event is to misunderstand miracles. This intensity of symbolic meaning in the miracle stories distinguishes New Testament miracles from their contemporary parallels.

The miracle motif, too, is still an elemental presence in our lives. It allows us to see reality under the aspect of the unexpected: nothing is so set in stone that events take place without any surprises. Appreciation of miracles does not depend on believing that the laws of nature can be suspended. But the miracle motif does go hand in hand with the promise that human desires are not ruled out from the start. A desire can be articulated in a prayer or in an outcry. Even in a hopeless situation, there is hope for a turnaround. Above all, such a motif has the power to bring people together, expressing the conviction that no one is ever totally abandoned. Even at the last moment, there can be a turn for the better. Even the hopeless prospect that all will not have bread to eat must not be the last word. Neither must an incurable disease move us to distance ourselves from others. Everywhere there radiates the certainty that even in extremities life is enfolded in the power of God. There is no fatalism. There is the elemental miracle of life.

Alienation

All life is lived at a distance from God and never does justice to the reality that brought it forth and sustains it. We are separated from God by sin and suffering, finitude and death, as well as by dark powers, and are therefore alienated from the wellspring of our own being.

One simple principle pervades the entire Bible: God is holy, eternal, and omnipotent, but sinful human beings are subject to death and threatened by powers at enmity with God. This contradiction demands explanation. It is contrary to God's intent in the creation of humankind. The primal history tells how sin entered the world. Beginning with the knowledge of good and evil, sin mounts to aggression against another human being in the murder of Abel—and reaches new heights in blood vengeance. The boundaries between God and humanity are repeatedly overstepped, as human social relationships are destroyed. The sons of God beget the giants (Gen. 6:1-4): here it is divine figures that overstep the boundary. Then human beings build the tower of Babel: here it is they who overstep the boundary. Sin means the loss of human fellowship and cooperative solidarity.

With the dawn of monotheism, the knowledge of sin becomes focused in one original sin: apostasy and the worship of other gods. The Deuteronomistic history (Joshua, Judges, 1–2 Samuel, 1–2 Kings) uses this perspective to structure the history of Israel: sin and apostasy, followed by punishment and repentance. It is up to humanity whether historical epochs come to a good or bad end. A sense of responsibility for history is vigorously inculcated; the conscience is trained. In counterpoint to the emphasis on responsibility in the Deuteronomistic history, the Priestly source that scholars discern in the books of the Torah affirms God's irrevocable promise to Israel: there is atonement for sin. In the postexilic period, sacrifices served primarily to efface guilt, the consequence of sin. The high point is the Day of Atonement, which blots out all the unknown sins of the people (Leviticus 16).

But neither the inculcation of responsibility nor priestly atonement through sacrifice solves the problem. Increasing ethical awareness makes God appear increasingly "alien." Job protests against the attempt to account for suffering through a heightened awareness of sin. He asserts his innocence, and only the revelation of a God who is "wholly other," who is infinitely superior, will silence him. Who is ultimately "wrong," Job or God, remains an open question. It is only clear that a mortal cannot challenge God, but also that God values contentious debate more than a rationalizing ascription of evil to human sin. The framework narrative of the book of Job presents a third possible explanation of evil: Satan appears as an accuser. Evil is ascribed to a demonic power neither divine nor human. But this possibility plays no role in the debate within the framework.

In the New Testament Satan has become a third force alongside God and humanity, an anthropomorphic token of the world's enmity as a hostile power. Thus, it explores all three—sin, Satan, and God—as possible sources of evil, as follows:

1. In the New Testament, the sense of sin is radically heightened—from the Baptist, who calls on all to repent in the face of God's wrath (Matt. 3:7-12), to Paul, for whom humanity as "flesh" is fundamentally hostile to God (Rom. 8:7).
2. Humanity is threatened by demons and hostile power, which Jesus overcomes through exorcisms (Matt. 12:28). They flee, but total victory awaits the resurrection. The exaltation of the risen Christ makes him Lord over all forces and powers (Rom. 8:31-39).
3. The New Testament, too, can see God as *deus absconditus*, the source of evil: the metaphor of the potter gives God the freedom to cast aside anyone, without any reason (Rom. 9:19-24).

In the major schemata of the New Testament, we find a balance among these three factors. Romans assigns the responsibility for evil to sin (Rom. 1:18-19; 5:12-14), the powers (8:31-39), and God (9:19-24)—but always with the knowledge that Christ has wiped out sin, vanquished the powers, and overcome the wrath of God.

Alienation is an elemental motif of life. It shows us how far removed we are from life as it should be—and this in our encounter with an infinitely precious reality: God as the absolute energy driving all that is good. Our modern mentality is more ready to understand alienation from God through finitude and suffering than through sin and guilt. Indeed, the modern era has witnessed a revolt against the sense of sin inculcated by the biblical tradition—often as a protest against an understanding of sin that associates it with sexuality. Nevertheless, a biblically "informed" sense of sin better accounts for our reality than does an optimism that refuses to consider a fundamental human flaw: the greater potential we have, the more we must view our inability to realize that potential as failure—both individually and globally. To use a metaphor: God and evolution have led us into the promised land of our small planet. It is up to us how—indeed, *whether*—we will live on this planet. The Bible presents this responsibility for history, as well as the failure to meet it, in sharp relief—but also the survival of those who have failed. What is true of history as a whole is also true of each individual's life story. Only a minority on this earth, we have the chance to shape our lives on the basis of our individual goals. For this very reason, our sense of failure is all the more intense, for we miscarry through our own frailty, not because of outward impediments. This motif of alienation also has a human aspect: it keeps us from self-righteousness. We all come short of what we would and, before God, should be. A sense of personal imperfection can link adults and children. Children in particular constantly have their imperfections called to their attention, while adults often preach to them a hollow "perfection." An elemental sense of alienation can be with us throughout our lives: all are far removed from what they truly should be, and hence far removed from God.

Hope

History is infused with hope for a new world that has already begun in the midst of this world. Christians are citizens of two worlds: while our *sarx* (body) imprisons us in the old world, through our *pneuma* (spirit) we live already in the new world that began with Jesus.

The Old Testament is the history of a steadily expanding promise. Even the first appearances of evil are seen in its light: Cain is assured that he will master sin (Gen. 4:7) and Noah is promised that a deluge will never again devastate the earth (9:15). Abraham is promised land and descendants (12:1-3). The prophets cite the saving acts of God in the past and promise that they will be "repeated" in the future: a new covenant, a new exodus, a new heart, or a new David—even a new heaven and a new earth.

Apocalypticism elaborates this expectation of a new world. The New Testament presupposes its vision of the world and humanity as an eschatological transition—before Easter as imminent expectation of the reign of God, which is beginning even in the present (Mark 1:14-15), after Easter as the belief that the new world has begun with Jesus' resurrection. In various ways, the whole New Testament is pervaded with this sense of transition between an old world and a new world.

1. For John the Baptist and Jesus, this sense of transformation takes the form of imminent expectation of God's reign. Their followers are on the threshold of the new world, which is about to dawn. This is what the Baptist means when he says that the ax is already lying at the root of the trees. Such expectations flared up repeatedly in primitive Christianity (Mark 13; Revelation)—especially in crises like that attested in the Apocalypse of John. Jesus himself could incorporate the Baptist's frustrated expectations in his message: the failure of the judgment predicted by John to arrive is a sign of God's mercy, giving people time to repent (Luke 13:6-9).

2. The realized eschatology of primitive Christianity after the cross and Easter goes a step further. It rests on the conviction that Christians have already crossed the threshold of the new world: they have passed from death to life (John 5:24; 1 John 3:14). They have now been transferred spatially to a different realm of being (Col. 1:13; 3:1-4; Eph. 2:1-7). They walk in "newness of life" (Rom. 6:4), live even now as a "new creation" (Gal. 6:15; 2 Cor. 5:17; Col. 3:10; Eph. 4:24), and already rise from the dead (Eph. 5:14). But they are affected by the forces of both the old world and the new: Christians are citizens of both worlds, torn between *sarx* as the power of the old world and *pneuma* as the vital force of the new (Rom. 8:5-11).

3. Saving history is a third possible way to express the transitional sense of primitive Christianity. It emerged among the third generation of early Christians from reconsideration of imminent expectation and realized eschatology. In Jesus salvation was imminent. The time before Jesus was a time of expectation, the time afterward a time of mission. The time of Jesus is the center of the time of fulfillment. This time of fulfillment has three parts; it was inaugurated by John the Baptist and it continues in the age of the church. Luke's two books present the story of this fulfillment with Jesus as the center of time. This division of time into periods emphasizes a central time of salvation.

In all these conceptions, hope for a fundamental transformation of all things determines the vision of the cosmos and of humanity. Just as the whole world must be renewed, so must humanity: God enables "newness of life" (Rom. 6:4) and rebirth (John 3:5; Titus 3:5). This parallelism between cosmic and human renewal can be called "participatory eschatology." The life of the individual takes part in a general renewal of the world. But this individual renewal is so important that it can be seen as a fundamental motif in its own right: conversion.

But before turning to that motif, let us glance at the motif of hope as an elemental theme. It appears to have been lost to humanity with the failure of faith in progress; in both the religious and the secular world, however, it survives every eschatological disappointment. Despite the frustration of utopian hopes for a great turn to a better world, we continue to paint images of peace with nature and among humankind, a world in which food, security, and education are equally available to all. And although we may be skeptical or even cynical about the possibility of increased justice and freedom, we do not infect our children with this resignation, as though there is something that warns us not to rob the younger generation of the chance to enter a better future. There remains an elemental hope, which it would be sacrilege to quench.

Conversion

Human beings enjoy the possibility of radical change. Just as the world must change to reflect God's will, so must the individual, who can begin a new life by being crucified with Christ and beginning a new life with him.

Within the Bible, there emerges the idea that individuals can radically reorient their lives and make a new beginning. They can turn away from God, but they can also return to God. The possibility of such change is associated with the development of monotheism. If the choice is between the one God and other gods, turning to God always means turning away from the many gods. Ancient polytheism, by contrast, made it possible to worship additional deities. The choice between true and false worship was introduced by Israel. It was this either/or that led to the notion of a fundamental conversion. Only in ancient philosophy do we find a certain analogy: it, too, was concerned with the choice between truth and error and a fundamental change in a person's life, to truth from error.

The prophets demanded conversion (repentance) on the part of the entire nation. In the preexilic prophets, the possibility of repentance and return often seems to be nothing more than a missed opportunity. After each of God's punishments, Amos repeats the refrain: "Yet you did not return to me" (4:6-11). Hosea complains: "Their deeds do not permit them to return to their God" (5:4; cf. Isa. 9:12). Jeremiah says that Israel is like a woman who has left her husband and gone to another: she cannot return to her husband (Jer. 3:1; cf. Deut. 24:4).

But how is such return possible? It will come only after an enormous outward and inward transformation. The outward transformation consists in God's punishment. After the catastrophe, a surviving remnant returns. Isaiah therefore programmatically named his son Shear-jashub, "A remnant returns" (Isa. 7:3; cf. Isa. 10:20-27; Ezek. 33:10-16; Zeph. 3:12-13; Zech. 8:1-8). The inward transformation consists in renewal through God. The penitential psalms had always prayed for such renewal: "Create in me a clean heart, O God, and put a new and right spirit within me. Do not cast me away from your presence, and do not take your holy spirit from me. Restore to me the joy of your salvation, and sustain in me a willing spirit" (Ps. 51:10-12). The exilic and postexilic prophets proclaimed this inward transformation as a future event: "A new heart I will give you, and a new spirit I will put within you, and I will remove from your body the heart of stone and give you a heart of flesh. I will put my spirit within you, and make you follow my statutes and be careful to observe my ordinances" (Ezek. 36:26-27; cf. 11:19; 18:31; Jer. 24:7).

In the New Testament, conversion in the sense of return to God becomes something entirely different: Gentile Christians did not return to the one and only God but turned to God for the first time, and in doing so turned their backs on everything they had previously valued. In the Old Testament, this conversion of the Gentiles is prefigured in the expectation that the Gentiles would come to Yahweh and to Zion in order to worship God (Isa. 2:2ff.; 45:18ff.; 60:1ff.; Zech. 8:20ff.; 9:6ff.). Jesus stands in this tradition when he voices the expectation that they will flood into the kingdom of heaven (Matt. 8:11-12). Christians did not just await such a conversion passively as a divine miracle but became active missionaries, so as to reach all the nations and win them to the faith. They used a wealth of images to described conversion: a call (1 Cor. 1:2), enlightenment (Heb. 6:4), transfer of power (Rom. 6:13ff.), redemption (1 Cor. 6:20), rebirth (John 3:1ff.). All these images emphasized the break between the old life and the new, because it meant a radical transformation for Gentile Christians, as great as the change from death to life. To be converted meant dying with Christ and living with Christ (Rom. 6:1ff.). It is not by chance that this interpretation of baptism as death makes its first appearance with Paul, the apostle to the Gentiles, who had to demand of his Gentile Christian communities a particularly radical departure from their previous lives.

The motive for conversion should not be fear of judgment but the joy of God in heaven. This is particularly apparent in Luke's parable of the Prodigal Son: "There will be more joy in heaven over one sinner who repents than over ninety-nine righteous persons who need no repentance" (Luke 15:7, 16). This joy is meant to be shared on earth. The crux in the parable of the Prodigal Son is whether the elder son (and the reader) will be open to sharing this joy. Whether such conversion was possible only once for each individual was disputed. The author of Hebrews remained convinced that repentance and return subsequent to conversion was impossible, but his was a minority view (Heb. 6:4ff.; 10:26ff.). The community discourse of Matthew already includes Christians in its exhortation to repent (Matt. 18:3, 12ff.). The letters in Revelation call on established churches to return (Rev. 3:5, 16, 21, and so forth). A readiness to repent and return is lifelong; it is not limited to a single point in time.

The motif of repentance and return is one of the most positive forces that can affect a life. For it says that you can fail time and again, but you can begin anew! People are not shackled to their transgressions forever.

They are not doomed irretrievably to end in the abyss. They can repent. They are born to be reborn. They suffer defeats to rise up again. The German poet Johann Wolfgang von Goethe, who was no Christian, described this motif as a life-sustaining force: "And so long you won't it quest, / This dying and rebirth, / You will be a dreary guest / Upon the darkling earth." The fundamental conviction that life can be renewed in the midst of life is an elemental certainty of the Christian faith. Those who grow up inwardly persuaded that they are born to be reborn—time and time again—approach life with different expectations than do others. But they also see their neighbors differently, as human beings who can repent. The chance to make a new beginning, time and time again, gives a new perspective on life, especially for children and young people. Here, too, we can speak of an elemental chance to repent, which we allow to all as we claim it for ourselves.

Exodus

It is not just individuals that are transformed by God's call, but whole groups—beginning with Abraham's exodus from his homeland and Israel's exodus from the foreign land of Egypt to the emergence of the New Testament community into a new world as followers of Jesus. In the Bible, renewal can affect an entire people. Repeatedly we encounter the notion that a people leaves one world to pioneer a new land and there establishes a new communal life. Departure and a blueprint for an alternative communal life—often sharply distinct from the "old world"—constitute the exodus motif of the biblical tradition.

Abraham was the first to leave his homeland. He had been promised that he would become a great nation, multiply, and be given land. Without any military conquest, in fact taking care to avoid conflicts, he entered the new land. The new life there was endangered by perils from within, not without: conflicts among brothers and kin. The conflict between Jacob and Esau threatens the promise. The Joseph novella shapes the conflict among brothers and shows that only forgiveness makes community possible.

The exodus narrative proper offers an alternative interpretation of Israel's origin to that in the patriarchal narratives: the people escape an oppressive regime, flee before the chariots of Egypt, and take the land by force of arms. In the desert, they are confronted with the will of God.

The Ten Commandments define the conditions for Israel's preservation of its freedom from "Egypt"—that is, from slavery. Besides the external threat, they now face the threat of apostasy from God: the story of the golden calf (Exodus 32) and the complaints of the people against Moses (Exodus 16–17; Numbers 11).

The return of the exiles from Babylon and the establishment of Judah as a temple state is the third great exodus in the Bible. Deutero-Isaiah had announced this return as a new exodus (Isa. 40:3ff.). The returnees wanted for the first time in history to make religious faith the basis of a commonwealth. They codified their traditions and made them a law of God, independent of any state. Although now for the first time the exclusive claims of the one and only God were legally binding, Jews tolerated diverse ways of life in the Pentateuch: hopes for a national restoration alongside the certainty that in the temple cult history had already found its culmination. A sacred commonwealth came into being that considered itself a world set apart from the world around it.

The New Testament community understands itself in its tradition as an exodus community. Following the model of the Old Testament exodus from Egypt (1 Cor. 10:1ff.), it forsakes existing society and sets out on a journey through history (Heb. 3:7ff.; 11:1ff.). It has a sense of embodying a different world. Those who belong to this community are nothing in the eyes of the world (1 Cor. 1:26ff.), where they are strangers and aliens (1 Peter 1:1ff.). And yet they, like political communities, constitute an *ekklesia*, a corporate "body," a people. But within it other rules apply than in the surrounding world.

In the modern world, the exodus motif still moves people to forsake traditional ways of living to explore new alternative ways—even beyond the boundaries of society. One of these exodus movements was the youth movement of the early twentieth century. The reform movements of the 1960s still had the intensity of an exodus. Naturally, their rebellion against authority no longer strikes a responsive chord today, when young people find that almost everything is permitted. The emancipatory impulse fades when no one knows what to be emancipated from or for. But the theme is timeless. People are poorer for having no experience of such pioneering movements. In every age, there is an elemental sense of a need to move on, which enables us in the present to apprehend and visualize the signs of a new world.

Substitution

All life is interwoven so closely that one life can take the place of another. What happens to one person happens also to others or benefits them. It happens vicariously for others. Animal sacrifice bears witness to the compulsion to live at the expense of others. Christ shows the alternative: to live on behalf of others.

Vicarious representation is a structure affecting all of life. What happens to one can happen analogously to all. Such representation is operative in many human transactions, not just in substitutionary sacrifice. In such sacrifice, however, this fundamental structure of human life is given concrete representation in a symbolic ritual. By synecdoche—whereby a single entity is used as a sort of shorthand expression of something larger—the victim represents those offering it, being identified either with the whole person or their possessions. In any case, the blood of the sacrificial animal represents life and is therefore given back to God by being sprinkled on the altar during the ritual. The Bible also draws on this concept independently of the sacrificial system: the Servant of the Lord suffers vicariously for the sins of many (Isaiah 53).

Vicarious representation is everywhere. Adam, as progenitor, represents humankind. All are formed in his image; his sin affects all. By analogy and contrast, Christ is the "progenitor" of the new humanity (Rom. 5:12ff.). Thus, he represents vicariously what should one day be. As the ancestor of Israel, Abraham is also the ancestor of the Gentiles. The righteousness reckoned to him will be reckoned to all (Rom. 4:1ff.) and will be a blessing for all nations (Gal. 3:6ff.)—provided that they are "descended" from Abraham through faith. He is a vicarious ancestor.

The motif of an emissary is a second variant of the representation motif. "Whoever sees me sees him who sent me" (John 12:45). This motif is used similarly of the disciples—"Whoever listens to you listens to me" (Luke 10:16)—and of children: whoever welcomes them welcomes Jesus, and whoever welcomes Jesus welcomes the one who sent him (Mark 9:37). A third variant is action on behalf of others: one can pray for others (Rom. 1:8), be baptized for others (1 Cor. 15:29), bear burdens for others (Gal. 6:2).

The notion of dying for others is embedded in a wealth of vicarious relationships. "One has died for all, therefore all have died" (2 Cor. 5:14). Through God's resurrection power, they are now a "new creation" (2 Cor.

5:17). Besides this "inclusive" representation, we find an "exclusive" representation in the New Testament: Christ became what we need not be—a sin offering (Rom. 8:3) and curse (Gal. 3:13-14). In a similar vein, Paul can say that death is at work in him that the community may have life (2 Cor. 4:12). But he can also say that life is made visible in him (4:11), preserving the analogy between him and the Corinthians. Statements about the vicarious role of Christ are similar: according to Paul, it is not simply his death that brings salvation, but his death overcome through resurrection. Christ "was handed over to death for our trespasses and was raised for our justification" (Rom. 4:25; cf. 5:10; 6:1ff.; 8:34). Those who have faith will also die and rise with Christ.

The motif of vicarious representation links us with others and with all creatures. Each living creature contains a piece of genetic code related to us. Each harbors the same will to live that we do. The suffering of other creatures is therefore always vicarious suffering as well—without which others could not live. The notion of vicarious representation acknowledges this fact. Among human beings it is an oppressive problem. All life lives at the expense of other life. Human beings battle each other for survival. The notion of vicarious representation holds this depressing fact before our eyes and makes the reverse possible: people can also live positively for each other and help others bear the burdens of life instead of imposing their own burdens on others. Here we discover something truly elemental. Children and young people also experience vicarious representation. On important occasions they must be represented by others. Their experience differs, depending on whether they see this vicarious action as beneficial or as suppressing their true selves. It is not for nothing that parents give their children hamsters to care for: children must vicariously protect the lives of their pets. Responsibility for others is a vicarious role. Children can experience even more deeply than we adults that their pets are related to them. We all have an elemental sense of mutual dependence.

Divine Indwelling

God comes to dwell in the real, sensible world. God is present in humanity through the Spirit, in Christ through incarnation, in worship through the sacraments. The church is the "house" in which God dwells, the "body" in which God is visible. The incarnation of God in Christ assures us once for all of God's presence with humanity—even in the midst of sin and suffering.

The Old Testament speaks of God's dwelling—above all as the indwelling of God's spirit or wisdom in chosen individuals (Wisd. 7:27) and the dwelling of God's name in the Temple. God dwells in the midst of Israel; one day the whole earth will be filled with God's glory (Ps. 72:19).

These ideas are developed in the New Testament—initially with reference to Christ: God's dwelling with humanity becomes the exclusive incarnation of the *Logos* in *sarx* (John 1:14; cf. Col. 2:9). Christ replaces the Temple (John 2:18ff.). He embodies the presence of God in the world.

Christians are spoken of similarly: their body is a temple in which dwells the Holy Spirit, sent from God (1 Cor. 6:19); they are "members of Christ" (1 Cor. 6:15). The Christian community is the house and temple of God (1 Cor. 3:16) as well as the "body of Christ" (1 Cor. 12:12ff.; Rom. 12:3ff.). In antiquity, the image of the body was commonly applied to a political community; early Christianity remythologized it by relating it to the mysterious presence of the risen Lord in his community. Therefore, the Christian community also embodies God's presence in the world.

Finally, the motif of dwelling includes belief in the sacramental presence of Christ—whether understood as a presence through remembrance, as the personal presence of the Lord inviting us to his Supper, as a social presence in the community, or as Christ's real presence in the bread and wine (John 6:51ff.). From the soil of texts that speak of God or Christ as "dwelling" grow reciprocal expressions leading to the mystical language of "being in Christ." Christians are in Christ (Rom. 8:1) and at the same time Christ is in them (Rom. 8:10). In the Gospel of John, Christ and God come to dwell in those who believe. They are in them, and those who believe are in Christ (John 14:20ff.). In 1 John 4:16, we even find a "mystical" text with reference to God: "God is love, and those who abide in love abide in God, and God abides in them."

The motif of dwelling says that God is present in the midst of life to sanctify it through his presence. This is an elemental experience even today. The world can take on a "sacramental" quality and become a transparent token of God's loving-kindness. Physical objects like bread and wine, a human individual, and the community of believers become loci of God's presence. The motif of dwelling enhances the corporeal reality around us and within us. But it also gives dignity to the beggar and the outcast: they are brothers of the Most High, in whom he is personally concealed. This motif of dwelling finds its boldest symbolic expression in the idea of incarnation: the deity has entered personally into a concrete human being, a total life with its highs and lows, with suffering and death. Children find it easy to experience realities not just as subjective images but as real phenomena with an increment of objective reality. The capacity to experience more than the sensible reality of the world about us permeates all of life as an elemental experience of depth—a more intense experience of reality with an ever-present dimension of depth.

Faith

God and salvation are revealed to us by faith as a total act of trust, through which we ground our lives on something outside us. At the center of all those through whom God speaks stands Jesus of Nazareth.

We meet the idea of faith in the Old Testament initially in the context of human belief in a statement or person (Prov. 14:15; 26:25; Gen. 45:26). This response of trusting faith is directed toward God in the Abraham tradition (Gen. 15:6) and in Isaiah (7:9; 28:16).

In the New Testament, which builds on Jewish tradition, this faith becomes a fundamental trust in God and Christ. There is a striking correlation between statements about faith and outward events. The New Testament speaks of the coming of faith and the coming of Christ (Gal. 3:23; Mark 2:17), the victory of faith and the victory of Christ (1 John 5:4; John 16:33), the omnipotence of faith and the omnipotence of God (Mark 9:23; 10:27). In the New Testament, faith becomes inward "judgment" even while the outward judgment of God remains (John 3:18; 5:29). Faith justifies in exactly the same way that God justifies. All this is more than shorthand: faith secures the personal center in God's outward saving act and in the person of the Redeemer. And the statements about it vary with the diversity of God's action.

Faith is rarely linked with creation in the sense of belief in the one and only Creator God (James 2:19; Heb. 11:3). Occasionally it resembles endurance, that is, fidelity and perseverance on the long road of history (Heb. 11:4ff.). More often it is trust in a sustaining divine power, exhibited through faith in prayer and miracles (Mark 2:5; 11:22-23; James 1:6; 5:15).

Above all, though, it is the faith to confess Jesus Christ that justifies and redeems (Mark 1:14-15; Rom 10:9; and others). Thus, it is related to belief in God, Christology, and ethics.

The motif of faith is almost the converse of the dwelling motif, in which the transcendent God pervades earthly reality; in faith, it is humans who transcend their finite reality so as to enter the sphere of divine reality, to find outside themselves a firm foundation, "the assurance of things hoped for, the conviction of things not seen" (Heb. 11:1).

The motif of faith is an existential motivation to affirm life, a courage to live grounded in trust in something over which we have no control. This trust is comparable to trust in a person. It always involves an element of risk. It is never possible to be certain in advance when we put our trust in a human being. The same is true of our relationship to the total system of reality. Here, too, we encounter something quite simple: a basic elemental trust with which everyone embarks on life. When this trust is broken, a dark shadow falls over life. In most cases, fortunately, it grows and develops in relationships with the child's closest attachment figures.

Love (Agapē)

Love establishes a positive relationship with God and with other human beings. Love makes every person our neighbor—whether through quest for the lost, welcome for strangers, or love of enemies. Here, too, Christ is the prototype of such life: his self-sacrifice is love of those who were God's "enemies."

While faith moves only from human beings toward God and Christ, and cannot be used in this sense for interpersonal relationships, God, Christ, and humanity are linked by love, in a structure of mutuality. The history of love of neighbors begins in the Old Testament. In the Holiness Code (Lev. 19:18) it is love of one's personal enemy, against whom it is wrong to take vengeance. Here, too, it already includes weaker individuals, who must be helped. And here, too, verse 34 extends it to love of resident aliens. In its first formulation, then, love of neighbors includes love of enemies, love of the powerless, love of strangers. Deuteronomy goes on to interpret our relationship with God as love—borrowing the terminology of the political loyalty that vassals owe their lords, here broadened to included the entire nation (Deut. 6:5).

Before Jesus, Judaism included both elements of the law of love (love of God and love of neighbor) in parenetic (that is, related to ethical instruction) series (*Testaments of the Twelve Patriarchs: T. Iss.* 5.2; *T. Zeb.* 5:1; and others). But only the Synoptic tradition joins them in a single command to love both God and neighbor—explicitly emphasizing and giving equal weight to both. We have here a characteristic extension beyond traditional limits, the core of which may well go back to Jesus: love of neighbors is radicalized and extended to love of enemies (Matt. 5:43ff.), love of strangers (Luke 10:25ff.), and love of sinners (Luke 7:36ff.). But Jesus never speaks of God's love. He understands love only as a human act.

It remained for Paul to speak of both divine and human love, although he does not ground human love by definition in God's love. Instead, he absolutizes love in a hymnic paean, as a personified power that emerges within the Christian community (1 Corinthians 13). For Paul, love stands in tension with innate human drives: it is the first of the fruits of the Spirit, which are contrary to the works of the "flesh" (Gal. 5:13-26). It also stands in tension with the coercive power of the state, which must insist on the vengeance that love eschews (Rom. 12:19ff.; 13:1ff.). It even stands in tension with religious charisms or gifts: "knowledge," prophecy, glossolalia (speaking in tongues or ecstatic speech) (1 Cor. 8:1ff.; 13:1ff.). Love is the highest charism, without which all the rest are worthless.

It was the Gospel of John that first conflated the two traditions of God's love and human love and explicitly made them mutually dependent: as God and Jesus loved the disciples, so they are to love each other (John 13:34-35; 15:9ff.). This love is limited to the internal life of the community, but it has significance for the surrounding world: the disciples will be recognized by their love. This love is far more than an ethical commandment. It conforms to a divine reality. In the Johannine corpus, we even find God defined as love (1 John 4:16). As a result of the centrality of love and its new status as a soteriological reality and an ethical commandment, the Johannine Jesus introduces the law of love (despite Lev. 19:18) as a "new commandment" (John 13:34-35). What is basically new is its centrality. It became the primary commandment of Christianity.

The *agapē* motif directs this energy of faith and trust toward our neighbors—not just the neighbors with whom we already have an affinity, but also those who differ from us, who are alien to us, even our enemies. Everything with a human face can approach us as an enemy, but every enemy can be transformed into a fellow human being. Everything with a human face can approach us as unmitigated misery and challenge us to transform this misery. The sense of fellowship is elemental.

Status Reversal

God puts down and raises up, makes the first last and demands our readiness to renounce status. From those who voluntarily renounce status to the point of self-stigmatization (in asceticism and martyrdom), there radiates a transforming power—and even more from Christ, the judge who is condemned, the priest who is sacrificed, the Lord of the universe who becomes a slave and on the cross lays the foundation for new life.

This fundamental motif appears already in the Old Testament interpretation of how God acts in history. In 1 Samuel 2:6-7, Hannah rejoices: "The LORD kills and brings to life; he brings down to Sheol and raises up. The LORD makes poor and makes rich; he brings low, he also exalts."

In the New Testament, Mary expresses this view of God's action in the Magnificat: "He has brought down the powerful from their thrones, and lifted up the lowly" (Luke 1:52). Mary herself is an example. Despite her "lowliness," she became the mother of the Messiah. The birth of the Messiah among the lowly is an expression of a fundamental change of status. The same motif appears in the New Testament picture of Jesus, who, though he was in the form of God, humbled himself even to death on the cross, to be exalted by God (Phil. 2:6ff.).

It also appears in ethical admonitions, as a demand for humility and renunciation of status or as a warning against pride (1 Peter 5:5). Whoever would be great in the Christian community must be ready to be everyone's servant, unlike those who exercise authority in the world (Mark 10:42ff.). Jesus himself sets the example. When he washes the disciples' feet, in the Gospel of John, he as Lord takes on the role of a slave, as teacher the role of a student, as a man the role of a woman (John 13:1ff.). It is even possible to view an entire Gospel as embodying this motif of change of status: he whom the angels served now serves all through the sacrifice of his life (Mark 1:13; 10:45).

Finally, we meet this motif in eschatology as the expectation that at the last judgment the last will be first and the first last (Mark 10:31). Martyrdom can also be considered a variation on reversal of status: Jesus prophesies the martyrdom of James and John (Mark 10:35ff.). Then the first will indeed become the last!

The motif of reversal of status is a major ethical value, second only to love of neighbors. In a hierarchical society, readiness to disregard one's own status and treat others without regard to their status is the only path to hierarchies with fundamental equality. In earlier times, this motif was called humility—willingness on the part of those of high rank to serve others. But "humility" was too often abused as a way of disciplining the lowly. Humility is above all a virtue of the powerful. It cuts through all considerations of rank and status. The humble must value all people regardless of their status and treat them equally—the exalted as well as the lowly. It is natural for children to wish the great to become small and the small to become great. Every human encounter between great and small requires the great to come down to the level of the small and raise them through respect. Here and in many other situations there is an elemental victory over status.

Judgment

Human beings are brought before God's judgment seat to answer for their deeds. God judges them by what they have done—on the basis of ethical standard. And Jesus himself is the judge and standard.

The judgment of God is closely linked with the kingship of God: just as the king gives justice to those who have few, if any, legal rights, so does God as the "Judge of all the earth" (Gen. 18:25). History is a tale of transgressions, of God's punishment and renewed mercy—from the dawn of time. The prophets grafted this forensic view of history deep in the consciousness of Israel. Apocalypticism extends God's judgment, making it universal: it includes not just the kings of the earth but all the host of heaven (Isa. 24:21). Even the dead are included (Dan. 12:2).

The New Testament develops this notion of cosmic judgment anthropologically: Paul describes what is required by the law as being written on the heart and the voice of conscience as an internal process in which the last judgment casts an anticipatory shadow (Rom. 2:12ff.). The idea of judgment is also associated with the redemption that has already come: in Christ God condemned sin in the flesh, so that in the Spirit Christians can fulfill God's demands (Rom. 8:3-4); for them there is no longer any condemnation (Rom. 8:1).

But this internalization of God's judgment in the present does not capture the unique nature of the judgment motif in the New Testament. The key is the tension between judgment and salvation. God appears in the New Testament both as the judge who condemns and as the power willing all to be saved (1 Tim. 2:4). This tension evokes three variants of the idea of judgment in the New Testament:

1. In the Synoptic tradition, judgment brings a paradoxical reversal: the first will be last (Matt. 20:16). It is lost sinners who have a chance.
2. The Deutero-Pauline epistles (that is, those written by others in Paul's name) relativize God's judgment through a tendency toward universal salvation. Its goal is the restoration of all things in Christ (Eph. 1:10). God's harsh judgment has no place here. Ephesians minimizes it.
3. The Gospel of John internalizes God's judgment. It takes place here and now in the decision whether or not to believe (John 3:17; 12:47). Jesus himself judges no one; people judge themselves through their unbelief (John 12:47). Even though this train of thought is never carried to its logical conclusion, it is true to say that the acquittal of the sinner in God's judgment nullifies the ethical rationality of retributive justice, while remaining tied to a forensic context.

The motif of judgment makes all living beings accountable to God, as though we were always standing before a judge who passes judgment on our thoughts, words, and deeds. Our culture is in revolt against this "tribunalizing" of life. But we have before our eyes the merciless tribunal of our own superegos rather than the tribunal of the Creator, who shows more mercy to the "works of his hands" than does the human conscience. Here, too, everyone who grows up in a healthy environment has an elemental experience of conscience.

Justification

The legitimation of being is as unfathomable as the existence of life itself. It is a creation *ex nihilo* that we receive in the same way that we "receive" our physical existence. We did not create ourselves. The basis of justification is the new creative act of God in Christ.

The motif of justification can be understood as an aspect of the notion of judgment, but it transcends the idea of judgment. In justification we encounter God as creator, who makes life begin again; as king, who establishes divine righteousness and justice in the world; as priest, who offers a vicarious sacrifice. Above all, however, we encounter God as love, accepting us unconditionally even though we are not acceptable. This motif is not limited to the conceptuality of justification.

It appears already in the primary history. Because "the wickedness of humankind was great in the earth, and every inclination of the thoughts of their hearts was only evil continually," God regrets ever having made humankind (Gen. 6:5-6). God destroys everything so as to save only Noah. After the deluge, however, God uses the same argument to assure the earth and humankind of existence and life: "I will never again curse the ground because of humankind, for the inclination of the human heart is evil from youth" (Gen. 8:21). Abraham's plea for Sodom (Gen. 18:16ff.) shows that God is ready to waive punishment for the sake of a few righteous individuals. But in Sodom there are fewer than ten righteous persons! The reversal from damnation to unmerited grace recurs repeatedly in the Bible. Hosea laments that the people are unwilling to repent and return to God. They are threatened with destruction like that which befell Admah and Zeboiim, two cities that suffered the fate of Sodom. Instead, it is God who repents and returns to God's people: "My heart recoils [lit. 'turns around'] within me; my compassion grows warm and tender. I will not execute my fierce anger; I will not again destroy Ephraim; for I am God and no mortal" (Hosea 11:8-9). It is God who is the one righteous person for whose sake wrath turns into mercy.

We also experience this reversal in the messages of John and Jesus. The Baptist proclaimed imminent judgment. It did not arrive: instead, Jesus appeared and proclaimed God's salvation.

Paul took the nucleus of this biblical message and elaborated it in the message of justification. By rights all are under God's wrath, because all have turned aside from God (Rom. 1:18ff.). But for the sake of one individual, Jesus of Nazareth, this "wrath" is transformed into unmerited "righteousness" (Rom. 3:21ff.). The concept of righteousness and justice behind Paul's thought is not the neutral justice that rewards the good and punishes the wicked, but the partisan justice that helps the poor and the weak—and here even stands on the side of sinners. This righteousness is more than righteousness: it is love and reconciliation; it does not simply produce a new forensic structure but establishes a new personal relationship. Beginning with chapter 5, Romans develops the message of justification along these lines. This development reaches its climax in Romans 8:31ff.: "Nothing can separate us from the love of God." The context remains forensic, but this love prevents it from ever coming to trial. There is no prosecutor: "Who will bring any charge against God's elect? It is God who justifies" (8:33). There is no longer any judge: "Who is to condemn? It is Christ Jesus, who died, yes, who was raised, who is at the right hand of God, who indeed intercedes for us" (8:34). All that remains is an advocate. It is not his death alone that is the ground of salvation but the victory over his death. The turnabout from wrath to righteousness, from enmity to reconciliation, results from the turnabout from death to life in the Christ event. Paul proclaimed this unconditional mercy of God universally. It embraces even the Gentiles who deny the one and only God. It embraces all who are still the enemies of God. Ultimately it is as unconditional as *creation ex nihilo*. Abraham's belief in the righteousness of God is belief in the God "who gives life to the dead and calls into existence the things that do not exist" (Rom. 4:17).

The motif of justification enshrines something of life's indestructibility. Despite every failure and shortcoming, there remains an ineradicable right to life, even when people believe that in certain situations (war, capital punishment, abortion, stem-cell research) it can be abridged. It is quite possible that in conflicts between two true goods we incur guilt ineluctably. But we sense the conflict only because there is within us an elemental affirmation of life that begins by affirming life fundamentally, even though this affirmation is but a faint echo of God's unconditional affirmation of life.

READING THE BIBLE WITH CHRIST AS CORE

In the two fundamental convictions and fourteen fundamental motifs I've just discussed, we find the "spirit" of the Bible. All the motifs have to do with Christ. None of them appears in just a single biblical theme: they all give structure to different kinds of content in the Bible. They are more formal, but also more basic than the traditional topics of Christian dogmatic theology. Here we have described the "grammar" of the symbolic language of the Bible, even though such a compendium of rules and regularities is not as precise as a linguistic grammar. But these motifs and convictions are sufficient to capture the spirit of the Bible. And it is through this spirit, I believe, that we can grasp the identity of the Bible through history. Furthermore, all these biblical motifs are or can become elemental motifs of human life: a sense of creatureliness, joy in nature's hidden wisdom, the experience of miracles, a feeling of alienation, hope, the chance to turn one's life around, readiness to set out, mutual solidarity, the experience of depth, fundamental trust, humanity, independence of status, conscience, affirmation of life. The biblical motifs mesh with the existential motifs of life and provide an interpretive framework for them. They all relate to an ultimate reality. They are motifs of faith as well as of life. Whoever internalizes them has in turn a motivation to search for them in the Bible. Here the Bible displays a motivational power that fuels itself.

These fundamental motifs (to which more could be added) are meant to help with two tasks. First, they aid us in understanding individual biblical texts. They clarify the goal of exegesis and interpretation. It is important, of course, not to apply these motifs mechanically: every text dealt with should open us to the possibility of expanding our list of "elementals." Second, the fundamental motifs can serve to evaluate whether the "spirit of the Bible" makes itself heard representatively in a selection of themes and texts. By themselves they are not sufficient for either task. As a resource for analyzing individual texts, they need to be combined with actual readings of the text itself. Let me give an example of what I mean.

The fundamental motifs I discussed above provide a tool for analyzing particular texts to identify what is most important in them. Let us use the creation story (Genesis 1–3) as an example. Here the fundamental biblical motifs are present in profusion. The *creation* motif stands out immediately: "In the beginning God created the heavens and the earth." The Hebrew word *bara'* ("create") appears only with God as subject. The phrase "the heavens and the earth" embraces the totality of all things. The next clause qualifies the statement a bit: "The earth was a formless void and darkness covered the face of the deep" (Gen. 1:2). Is there a formless chaos in addition to the heavens and the earth? In the background lurks the originally mythological notion that God had to battle this chaos to bring the world into being. Here, however, in contrast to other myths, God does not engage in a battle but creates through this word alone.

Creation involves *separation*. God separates light and darkness, the heavens and the earth, plants and animals, man and woman. All these separations take place consecutively, rising from inorganic matter to human beings. The world is structured. It has order and hierarchy. The *wisdom* motif shapes the order of the days of creation. Each time the text states that "God saw that it was good" (Gen. 1:9, 25, 31), this affirmation is meant to find an echo in the reader or listener. This world is in principle orderly and good: it is not chaos, but a setting for life.

The second creation account (Gen. 2:5ff.) concentrates on the human world. In the creation of man and woman, the *agapē* motif appears in elemental form: Adam looked for a partner among all the other creatures, without success. Only the woman created from his rib is his equal: "This at last is bone of my bones and flesh of my flesh" (Gen. 2:23). Therefore, he is filled with desire for her and becomes one flesh with her. When he leaves father and mother (contrary to the practice of the narrator's patriarchal environment), the unruliness of sexual desire is plain. This desire is more than sexuality. The source of joy is experienced by all of us in every person we experience as our kin, as bone of our bone and flesh of our flesh.

The first human couple is given a garden to cultivate. But they are forbidden to touch the fruit of two trees: the tree of life, and the tree of the knowledge of good and evil. And therein lies a paradox. For every individual aware of any commandment knows at least to distinguish good from evil. But we want to understand why the prohibition exists. And we can do that only by tasting the evil consequences of transgressing the commandment. The "fall" is a narrative realization of the *alienation* motif. We human beings share with God the knowledge of good and evil, but not life itself. We are similar enough to God to feel related through our knowledge of good and evil, and therefore to feel all the more deeply our distance from God in our finitude and mortality. What this means concretely is that if we lived in a sheltered garden without any experience of the world, we would not need to scrape out a living by the sweat of our brow, even if we needed to cultivate the garden. It is not labor as such but its drudgery that is a mark of our distance from God. If we lived forever, we would not need to rear a new generation. The labor of bearing and raising children reminds us of our distance from God, our loss of life.

There is much more to discover in the rich and dense text of the creation story. But our purpose here is only to show how to identify in texts engaging or motivating aspects that arise from the text itself—not primarily as potential applications to contemporary problems. It is important to remember that just as learning English grammar cannot replace reading Shakespeare, so analysis of the fundamental motifs of the Bible cannot replace reading its various and vivid texts. The fundamental motifs are important for identifying what is most important in the wide range of possible interpretations and extensions of the biblical tradition.

As a second example for the identification of elemental motifs in biblical material, we use the New Testament parable of the laborers in the vineyard (Matt. 20:1-16). Between morning and evening, the owner of the vineyard hires four groups of laborers to work in his vineyard. To the first group he promises to pay a denarius; to the second group he promises to pay "whatever is right"; the last two groups hired receive no explicit promise. In the end, however, he pays everyone, beginning with the last, the same as those in the first group. This evokes a protest on the part of the first group, who correctly point out that they have worked longer than the others. They insist that it is unjust to pay them the same as the last. In response, the owner appeals, first, to his own freedom—"Am I not allowed to do what I choose with what belongs to me?" (in the ancient world, doing whatever one chooses is a common formula for freedom)—and, second, to his generosity—"Or are you envious [literally: 'is your eye evil'] because I am generous?"

This parable presents a collision between two notions of reward: one is based on the principle of distributive justice, so that reward is proportional to performance; the other is based on the principle of generosity, so that reward is proportional to need (a denarius being a day's wages). These are the elemental structures immediately apparent in the text. Behind them stands "love," one of the fundamental biblical motifs, a love that is extended here to those who are less deserving. To us in the modern world, the parable instinctively recalls experiences of joblessness and a living wage—and here, too, we find tension between reward based on performance and universal support based on need. In this sense, the elemental experiences brought into play by this text are obvious. With regard to the younger generation, one could say that two stages of moral development are represented: a *conventional stage* that considers whatever conforms to the rules to be good, and a *postconventional stage* that frees itself from strict obedience to the rules for a benevolent end. Even if the owner of the vineyard is a stand-in for God, his actions are based on ethical criteria. In the context of Bible study, the parable could be used to promote the transition from a conventional stage of moral judgment to a higher stage of freedom: God acts freely, at the highest stage, beyond conventional notions.

All this is obvious. But the collision between benevolence and justice, between reward based on performance and reward based on need, can be assigned not just to different stages of moral (and religious) development, but also to different social subsystems, whose differences are within childhood experience. Equal reward independent of ability and performance would be quite unexceptionable in the context of a family, where all the members receive according to their need regardless of their performance. The head of the household has clandestinely become a father. He does not behave as in an economic context but as in a family, where parents love all the children equally—and lesser performance does not mean less food on the plate. In this case, we would not find here a development from an inferior to a superior morality, but a conflict between two settings. And the theological conclusion would be: God does not treat people like an employer does but like a father—and God is free to do so.

Alongside close reading of individual texts, the kind of Bible study I want to promote involves an endeavor to grasp the whole. The Bible is a labyrinth of books and texts. And yet we can bring some order to it if we know what to pay attention to: literary forms and theological motifs. Thus, we come to the use of these motifs as criteria for focusing our attention.

FORMS AND THEMES

Bible study should include a representative selection of the most important types and genres of biblical texts as well as texts and themes typical of various epochs, as immanent in the Bible itself: texts representing the primal history, the patriarchal period, the wilderness period, the period of the judges, the period of the monarchy, and so forth. The most important books (such as Genesis, Isaiah, Job, the psalter, the Synoptic Gospels, John, the major Pauline epistles) should also be represented by typical texts.

As always, form criticism merits special attention. More is involved than just a complete list of individual forms. In the sequence of dominant forms used in the Bible, we find a certain logic, which may be outlined briefly. In narrative texts, myths, sagas, novellas, historical narratives, vitae, anecdotes, and legends do not simply appear side by side or in combination. Instead, we find in the Bible a development that valorizes history as the setting of the decisive encounters between God and humanity—and the fulfillment of this setting through the history of Jesus of Nazareth in the New Testament. The overall history constitutes the framework in which God and God's people (representing all humankind) engage in dialogue.

Within this history, we can observe an increase in the use of forms that concentrate on a single figure. The books of the Pentateuch are called the books of Moses. Their focus, however, is not on Moses but on the people of Israel. None of the historical books deals exclusively with a single king. The Succession Narrative is a story of two kings, Saul and David. The Court History presents the transition from David to Solomon. A book is devoted to each of the prophets, but the prophet's life is recounted only fragmentarily; the focus is on the prophet's words. Only in the New Testament do we find a genre that concentrates on the life and death of a single figure: the story of Jesus of Nazareth in the Gospels. This genre, a vita centered on an individual, was alien to Judaism (Philo's *Life of Moses* is an exception), but it was common in the Gentile world. In the Bible, its very form clearly marks the culmination of a long dialogue between God and humanity. The second core belief of the primitive Christian faith, concentration on the Redeemer, is thus recorded in the language of biblical forms.

More can be said about the "form-critical" shape of this story. From God's side, the dialogue is advanced in commands and promises. The commands occur in two forms: as general commandments in the Torah and as specific messages conveyed by the prophets. The biblical command-ments appear in three great legal corpora: the Covenant Code, Deuter-onomy, and the Holiness Code. They all emphasize the Decalogue: the Ten Commandments given directly to the people without Moses' media-tion. All the other commandments (and hence all the law codes men-tioned above) are mediated by Moses. Among them we may emphasize the social commandments in the Holiness Code, including love of neighbors (Lev. 19:18). Here we are dealing with general commandments. They are all embedded in a framework shaped by the exodus motif. The First Commandment refers explicitly to the exodus: "I am the Lord your God, who brought you out of the land of Egypt, out of the house of slavery" (Exod. 20:2). Thus, all God's commands are given a historical dynamic. They are signposts on the way toward an unknown future, of which only one thing is clear: it is not to be retreat into slavery and dependence. All the commandments serve the cause of liberation.

On the other side, the prophets address specific situations with concrete messages. In the preexilic prophets—Amos, Hosea, and Jeremiah—these are linked with warnings of disaster; in the later prophets, they are linked increasingly with promises of salvation, as illustrated above all by Deutero-Isaiah. Here God's commands are set in a framework shaped by the motifs of judgment and hope. Commandments and prophecies dramatize this in dialogue form: God works within it through the divine word, in the twofold structure of command and promise.

The human response finds expression in several genres. It, too, makes use of various forms: psalms express both lamentation and praise in great diversity. Here we see into the hearts of the faithful in the Old Testament—their despair, their consolation, their hope and assurance. To this day the emotional intensity of their language is gripping, even though we know that generations have labored over them, leaving their trail in conventions of lamentation and joy. The motif of alienation permeates the psalms of lamentation in expressions of human despair, the motif of faith in confessions of trust and assurance.

The distance between God and humanity is treated differently in the light of the wisdom motif. Wisdom articulates questions and reflections, admonitions and aphorisms; it lives on the assurance of a background order to which the successful individual must conform. In wisdom literature, the debate between God and humanity becomes increasingly a debate among human individuals. In two genres, this interpersonal dialogue is formative. The questions raised by wisdom are discussed in the dialogue between Job and his friends. Here we find interpersonal debate, a genre unique in the Old Testament. In the New Testament Epistles, people communicate with each other in a very different way. In both genres, reflection on God's justice is pushed to its limit. Job insists on his innocence; Paul insists (in Romans) on universal human guilt. In both cases, the solution rests in God's hands. Job acknowledges that the relationship between guilt and recompense is unfathomable. Paul proclaims that the relationship between guilt and recompense has been annulled by the universal justification of sinners.

Throughout the Bible, every genre is set within a dialogue between God and humanity. The Bible does not contain a "salvific history" with a hidden plan that gradually leads to its goal, but it does contain a dialogic history that remains open as it progresses. Each of these biblical genres continues the dialogue with a new accent. The method of form criticism has opened our eyes to this dialogue. It has been a productive technique for achieving an exemplary reduction of the "biblical material." That is, reading one example of a genre is sufficient for understanding the basic literary structures of all analogous texts. In the search for what is elemental in the Bible, however, we cannot limit ourselves to basic literary structures. The search for exemplary texts cannot be satisfied with simply another outline of biblical form criticism; while it may yield a set of form-critically representative texts on the one hand, it also should offer, on the other hand, texts displaying the core convictions and fundamental motifs of the Bible. These may be arranged chronologically, either by the periods immanent in the Bible itself or by those identified by scientific scholarship. The deep grammar of the Bible's symbolic language will be recognized where its "rules" are reflected in texts belonging to various genres and periods.

An increasing emphasis on interpersonal dialogue can be noted in the Bible itself. In the late Old Testament period, biblical literature becomes open to dialogue with the surrounding cultures. The evidence is in the short book of Jonah, Job, and other wisdom literature. This dialogue must be updated to the present. In addition to asking about the "elementals" of the Bible, we must also ask about biblical resources for dialogue.

CHAPTER 4

The Bible in Dialogue
with a Pluralistic World

What aspects of the Bible promote dialogue in a pluralistic world? If asking about what is elemental in the Bible reduces the content of the Bible to a few fundamental statements, asking about its contribution to human dialogue draws attention to its diversity. We begin with the observation that the Bible comprises many books and many statements: universalistic creation stories and accounts of humankind's earliest history set alongside nationalistic accounts of the occupation of Canaan, the peaceful patriarchal narratives set alongside the bellicose book of Judges, imprecations against enemies in the Psalms set alongside love of enemies in the Sermon on the Mount, the eroticism of the Song of Songs set alongside the asceticism of Paul, the pessimism of Ecclesiastes set alongside the optimism of early proverbial wisdom.

Now one might say the entire Bible varies the same message to suit the situation. Different circumstances demanded different responses. But this (moderately) harmonizing approach cannot be sustained. In the Bible, every voice evokes a countervoice. The book of Jonah dissents from nationalistic prophecy, the pessimism of Ecclesiastes attacks classical wisdom, Jesus' "But I say to you" in the Sermon on the Mount corrects the revelation at Sinai, the Gospel of Matthew criticizes the Gospel of Mark by depicting Jesus as an observant Jew. The Bible includes internal dialogue, the interpretation of which continues to this day in different denominations and schools of thought. Its internal differences legitimize the diversity of Christianity; its unity legitimizes ecumenical dialogue.

Dialogue with other religions also begins in the Bible—not just as polemic against other "inferior" religions but as a search for common roots: Was Yahweh not also the God of the Midianites (Exodus 18)? Was

Yahweh not also the God of Job, a devout Gentile in the land of Uz (Job 1:1)? Did not the Ninevites also hearken to God's voice? Did not God even choose Cyrus, the Persian king, as God's "messiah" (Isa. 44:4—45:8)? The God of the Bible is the God of all people (Rom. 1:18ff.; 3:29). Dialogue among religions begins in the Bible!

This applies even to dialogue with secular interpretations of life. It is true that the biblical world knows nothing of a denial of God's existence, but we do find a practical denial of God's power to act. This is what the wicked and foolish mean when they say in their hearts, "There is no God" (Ps. 10:4; 14:1). The Wisdom of Solomon attacks the ungodly, whose position recalls Ecclesiastes (Wisd. 1:16—2:24). They say, "For we were born by mere chance, and hereafter we shall be as though we had never been" (Wisd. 2:2). That is the basic thesis of a potentially atheistic worldview, even though it is not worked out in detail.

In the modern world we must continue these internal dialogues of the Bible. For the Bible is no longer *the* book on which our culture builds consensus; its reception differs widely in various subcultures. It competes with other traditions. It has been a long time since the younger generation entered a world with no alternatives. Young people are confronted with religionless interpretations of life, non-Christian religions, and other Christian denominations. In this situation, the relevance of the Bible must be demonstrated in dialogue with secularization, interfaith dialogue, and interconfessional or interdenominational dialogue. An appreciative study of the Bible cannot conduct these dialogues in a vacuum. These kinds of studies must make it clear that participation is meaningful because such open dialogue can shed new light on the Bible.

The Bible in Dialogue with Contemporary Secular Culture

Secularization aggravates an internal contradiction in religions. Religions stand for the whole, but are excluded from certain domains (for example, economics). They nevertheless have a role to play. Secular institutions assume conditions that they cannot produce and that ultimately they even destroy. For instance, economics is based on sanctity of contracts and a willingness to perform: both are beyond price. Cheating is profitable in the short run, as long as the majority of people do not cheat. Economic criminals take advantage of the morality they subvert. Refusal to perform is a parasite on the willingness of others to perform. The situation is similar in politics. The democratic state rests on a legitimation that it cannot itself provide. Recognition of each individual cannot be created by legislative fiat. In politics, too, abuse of power is parasitic on the civility of others who are not prepared to sacrifice everything to stay in power. The ability to accept such contradictions means the ability to accept that sometimes it is the "wicked" who prosper rather than the "righteous," as Psalm 73 complains. The conviction that justice and civility are nevertheless better demands personal adherence to norms that go beyond utilitarianism. It demands a realization on the part of the "righteous" that they, too, are not perfect (and a sufficient sense of humor to put up with this imperfection in themselves and others). This approach to life can be grounded "religiously" through the acceptance of something absolute and unconditional. Without this conviction, the everyday world begins to erode. If commitment to truth lasts only while it pays, it soon evaporates. If helping makes sense only in expectation of help in return, it soon becomes nonsense. If forbearance is practiced only when it entails no disadvantage, it soon dies out. In a secular society that officially wants life (and education) to reflect a morality that unofficially it often disclaims, religion therefore continues to play a significant role: it points out these contradictions and enables internal resistance to them. In a society dominated by economics, it is therefore "functional" for religion to criticize the reduction of life to economics, thereby becoming "dysfunctional": without the subversive choice between God and mammon (Matt. 6:24), the dictatorship of mammon would be intolerable. But no religion can ground itself on its function, but only on its meaning. Therefore, the discussion that follows will not deal with the paradoxical function of a functionless religion, but rather its power as an interpretation of life.

The Bible relates everything to God, a preexistent wellspring of meaning to which people respond with their lives. All the fundamental motifs are adaptive structures relating to God's hidden reality enabling contact with it. The core convictions of the Christian faith, belief in a Creator and Redeemer, differ sharply from the secular worldview. Secular humanism holds that humanity itself projects the spark of meaning into a meaningless world. But religious humanism knows that the spark of meaning was conveyed to us and lights its fire within us. For religious humanism, giving meaning to the world and to human life is the continuation of a theme that is given to us, on which we play our own variations through-out our lives. For a religious person, therefore, all of life is a response to God, a preexistent wellspring of meaning that humanity did not create. One must decide between this belief and the unbelief convinced that it is humanity that brings meaning to the world, and no grounds can be cited for this decision. Of course (contrary to many hasty theological protests), the eye could not see the sun if it were not already adapted to the sun. There are signs in human life that point to God (as a preexistent wellspring of meaning behind reality). But it is also true that the sun must interact with the eye if it is to see. Without the sun's "self-disclo-sure" through its rays, eyes, though perfectly adapted to sunlight, could not see it! There are times when the sun is eclipsed—and, in the present day, times when God is eclipsed. But it is impossible to read the Bible without an understanding of what it means to speak of God. And even when God is silent (and human thoughts merely circle around God, as in wisdom literature), the divine is present. Therefore, we repeatedly face the crucial question: Is it possible to interpret this talk of God to secular contemporaries without making them converts?

Faith in God and Secular Experience

Are there ideas in the secular worldview that are convergent with the first premise of the biblical faith? The answer is less difficult than many think: when God is not the mystery behind all things, the place of God is taken by reality per se or "being." That in our everyday lives as well as in our most nuanced theories we have access only to reality as it appears to us, not to reality itself, is undeniable. What is true of our senses and intellect, however, need not be true in itself. Therefore, a secular worldview is also able to speak of an "ultimate reality." In dealing with this reality, such a worldview repeatedly leads to attitudes and modes of behavior that are analogous to religion in their manifestation. I will cite two examples, one from philosophy and one from literature.

Many modern philosophies view "being" as an entity that both reveals itself and withdraws. In Martin Heidegger's philosophy, a call issues from Being that awakens us and pulls us from the oblivion of our inauthentic lives. This Being employs us as its "guardians" or "shepherds," so that we live our lives in service of a mandate not of our own making. When we go on to hear of "reverence for Being" and an expectant "devotion" to

Being (in the sense of a meditative "thinking about Being"), there can be no doubt: here "Being" occupies a quasi-religious position, even though this philosophy of Being is not associated with a community and does not find expression in rituals and mandatory lifestyles. That many theologies identify God with "Being itself" confirms our observation that we are dealing with convergent trains of thought.

The second example comes from poetry. In terms of his worldview, Rainer Maria Rilke could be called a monist with anti-Christian leanings.[1] In Rilke's case, of course, such categorizations are far too schematic, for he trusted that his poetry would transform the world into a religious homeland and, like those of Orpheus himself, enchant the natural realm. He wrote poems that many have interpreted within the framework of Christian traditions and thus misunderstood, albeit productively. I recall how one of our religion instructors quoted the following poem from Rilke's *Book of Hours* with deep personal emotion:

> I live my life in widening rings
> which spread over earth and sky.
> I may not ever complete the last one,
> but that is what I will try.
>
> I circle around God's primordial tower,
> and I circle ten thousand years long;
> And I still don't know if I'm a falcon,
> a storm, or an unfinished song.

Only at the end of this poem might one hear the voice of the poet himself, whose song not only responds to God but gives him life. In another poem from the *Book of Hours*, he presents the image of God as a great cathedral under construction: "We are workers: apprentices, journeymen, masters, / we build you, the great high nave...." These artisans are building God. The poem ends with the words: "Only when the darkness falls will we release you straight, / as your coming contours dim. / God, thou art great." Is all this just religious window-dressing? Just self-transfiguration on the part of the poet? Or do we hear the voice of primordial mystical devotion? Do we not encounter here a belief in the creative word that has deserted religion for aesthetics?

Throughout our culture we find such hints of religious experience. They can be viewed within the framework of a theory of secularization, in which case they are echoes of a vanishing world. But they can also be seen as irritants to a secular sensibility that rejects its self-concept, in which case they are recollections of reality. In any case, they are what several scholars have called "traces of the word." And they are of great significance for an open, public reading of the Bible.

I believe that it is legitimate to point out such experiences that challenge our secular worldview, that irritate it and fracture it. These experiences also make themselves heard in the Bible, where they are interpreted as experiences of God. They can be described as experiences (1) of transcendence, (2) of contingency, and (3) of resonance; many people have such experiences without relating them to God. First they must be shaped and interpreted by the three transcendental categories of *the absolute, the eternal,* and *responsibility.* (Those cognitive acts that we perform in order to have any experiences at all are what we term "transcendental"; they are the internal conditions that make experience possible. Something is "transcendent," by contrast, if it lies beyond our thought or experience.) The Bible contains graphic images that help us picture these categories. *The absolute* appears as the apodictic law given at Sinai (Exod. 20:1ff.). *The eternal* comes alive in the psalmist's invocation of the God who was before the mountains were brought forth and the earth and the world were made (Psalm 90). Human *responsibility* is pictured as an accounting demanded by the eschatological judge to whom all deeds are known (Rom. 2:6-11). Of course, these experiences and categories are not limited to the language of the Bible, for people can relate to an ultimate reality in a variety of languages. But without the tradition of an existing language to express them they melt away, whether they are philosophical or religious, Christian or non-Christian. The Bible provides a language, tested over time, by which they can be shaped.

But now to the three fundamental religious experiences. I am well aware how unusual it is to attach much importance to such experiences. It would require a comprehensive theory of religion to justify them. What follows can only be an outline.

1. The Experience of Transcendence. We know that the everyday world in which we live is part of a larger whole. Our "world" is not reality per se.

It is only a phenomenal world that we have constructed and interpreted; it depends on our senses and our brain. We know very well that in picturing reality we are both receptive and productive. To the extent that we produce our reality with our epistemological tools, we can be wrong; to the extent that we process it receptively, we stay in contact with it. Depending on our philosophy, we may lend more or less weight to the productive factor. In any case, reality per se eludes us. At this point we have experiences of transcendence, even today. In our efforts to understand reality, we encounter something beyond our grasp, whether we call it "God" or "reality per se." The transcendent character of this ultimate reality is always the same.

Of course, we can decide that the difference between appearance and reality is trivial. Since we can make effective use of the phenomenal world through our technology, we can view reality per se as a black box that behaves according to our calculations even though we do not understand its internal mechanism. Since we shall never be able to compare our ideas and theories with this reality—to do so we should have to step outside our own consciousness—we cannot even know whether our hypotheses and constructions might actually be correct. Since the difference between appearance and reality is unimportant for our daily lives and our technology, we can simply set it aside and turn to what we actually can know and do! This attitude is quite self-consistent. But it is convincing only if we are content with a relationship to reality based on technological mastery. If we are interested not simply in mastering reality but in living in harmony with it, not simply in changing it but in changing ourselves to do it justice, the question of the reality beneath our everyday world brings us face to face with the abyss of transcendence. We feel it most intensely in the failure of our thought to grasp it, as the wave feels the rock on which it breaks.

The Bible provides us with a wonderful language for this experience. It does not speak of the transcendence of reality or being, but the preeminence of God. But in it both are conjoined: God and being, God and reality. Here God presents Godself as "I am who I am" or "I will be who I will be" (Exod. 3:14). The language emphasizes God's transcendence: "For my thoughts are not your thoughts, nor are your ways my ways, says the LORD. For as the heavens are higher than the earth, so are my ways higher than your ways, and my thoughts than your thoughts"

(Isa. 55:8-9). The prohibition of images—physical idols—conveys the fundamental impossibility of representing the "wholly otherness" of the deity, which frustrates all attempts to visualize it. It immediately follows the First Commandment: "You shall not make for yourself a likeness, whether in the form of anything that is in heaven above, or that is on the earth beneath, or that is in the water under the earth. You shall not bow down to them or worship them" (Exod. 20:4-5).

2. The Experience of Contingency. The same transcendence that radically evades our knowledge is experienced directly by our consciousness in extraordinary proximity, because it pervades everything and is present in everything. We ourselves are a piece of reality per se, although it evades our grasp no less within us than everywhere else. We *are*, even though our knowledge of what we truly are is inadequate. In one respect, however, we have an immediate consciousness of our being: we are contingent. Like all reality, from the most distant galaxy to the tiniest quark, we exist by chance, not by necessity. It is an inexplicable miracle that we exist, and not nothing. This miracle pervades us every moment and even includes the thinking by which we ascertain it. This omnipresent contingency is the second source of religious experience. Here it is not the contrast between being and appearance that is a source of religion, but the contrast between being and nothing. Everything that exists could also not exist. Everything that exists will someday not exist. Of course, it is possible to trivialize this experience. We might say: indeed, it is inexplicable that anything at all should exist and not nothing. But there is no mystery here, certainly no divine mystery. It is a trivial fact, irrelevant to our thought and action. But it is certainly not trivial that we return to nothing. And that facing our return to nothing we passionately affirm being—with thanksgiving for existence every day and every hour. Although we often shrink from our passing into nothing, we sometimes experience a great sense of peace when we think of this cessation of existence.

The experience of transcendence and contingency together is crucial. In experiences of transcendence, being eludes us. We always fail to grasp it. In experiences of contingency, however, it is closer to us than our very selves. It encompasses our selves. It emerges as an all-defining reality. It pervades our innermost being. The Bible also has a powerful language for expressing this contingency of existence. The chance and transitory nature of existence takes the form of a lament: "All people are grass, their constancy is like the flower of the field. The grass withers, the flower fades, when the breath of the LORD blows upon it; surely the people are grass. The grass withers, the flower fades; but the word of our God will stand forever" (Isa. 40:6-8). "You sweep them away, they are like a dream, like grass that is renewed in the morning; in the morning it flourishes and is renewed; in the evening it fades and withers" (Ps. 90:5-6). But there is also joy in one's own existence: "For it was you who formed my inward parts; you knit me together in my mother's womb. I praise you, for I am fearfully and wonderfully made. Wonderful are your works; that I know very well. My frame was not hidden from you, when I was being made in secret, intricately woven in the depths of the earth. Your eyes beheld my unformed substance. In your book were written all the days that were formed for me, when none of them as yet existed" (Ps. 139:13-16).

3. The Experience of Resonance. What manifests itself in experiences of transcendence and contingency can be trivialized and ignored. If we do not do so, it is because we sense a challenge in these experiences. Reality per se "calls" to us, as though we should have to sacrifice all our notions and ideas when they prove to be insufficient to grasp it. The wonder of being and nonbeing "speaks to us" and fills us with gratitude, as though our lives would be inadequate if we did not react with deep emotion. Both types of experience are thus saved from trivialization if we experience them as *resonance*—if in this reality we encounter something profoundly related to us that strikes a resonant frequency within us. "Resonance" can be understood as a cosmic principle that binds the universe together—from the smallest particles to the most complex organisms. Something in the surrounding reality seems to echo us, and we can understand ourselves as echoing this something.

Such experiences of resonance are the third source of religious experience. Their significance can be illustrated by the problem of grounding ethical norms. We can never derive an ethical principle from observed facts. Therefore the "world" as the embodiment of all that is actually the case can never provide normative motivation for our actions. How then did our ethos come into being? Probably some groups proved superior to others on account of their morality. They had the better chance for survival. They and their ethos therefore endured. But groups with great

internal cohesion not only had a better chance for surviving wars and crises, they became so attractive that they won even their enemies to their
way of life. Our ethics is the product of two peoples, Jews and Greeks,
who converted their Roman rulers to their culture and religion (if we
may take Christianity as a variant of the Jewish religion). The victory of
their ethos was not the result of social Darwinism. What prevailed was
not a morality that was the most effective means of killing others and
offered the best chance to survive. The ethos that prevailed was one that
could attract strangers, that eliminated destructive elements through
trial and error and provided a practical way of life. But as we know only
too well, the functionality of an ethos does not validate it. No matter how
many people are convinced that they should conform to certain rules,
the result is not normative force but merely social pressure to conform.
The fundamental principle remains: imperatives do not follow from facts.
Standards accepted by many are not necessarily norms. It is therefore a
huge leap from the observation that a particular ethos has proved its
worth and functionality to personal commitment to that ethos. Such a
commitment means inward affirmation. It means adherence to it amid
all the conflicts of life, practicing it in spite of all the detriments it brings,
readiness to sacrifice one's life rather than one's convictions.

How is this leap from the observed validity of an evolved ethos to
normative conviction possible? There is just one imperative—more than
an imperative—that makes it happen: you must live, and you may live.
If we are convinced of this imperative, then the imperatives that make
life possible follow by inescapable logic. The affirmation of one's own life,
the lives of others, and the world go hand in hand. To affirm my own
existence is at the same time to affirm the processes that over millions of
years have created the chemical bonds that constitute my entire being.
To affirm my own existence is at the same time to affirm the thousands
of years of history that have produced me and the other human beings
without whom I could not live. But where is it that we hear this fundamental imperative—you must live, and you may live? We hear it in
thanksgiving for life and affirmation of the existence of *something* rather
than *nothing*. This is the fundamental religious experience. Anyone who
is sensible of it can experience reality as a great ethical force, as a glowing
fire of love that becomes the flames of hell when resisted. Such a person experiences in it the God of Sinai as a center of concentrated ethical

energy. When we are gripped by this unconditional affirmation of life as the will that that *something* should exist and that we should exist in the midst of all things, then it becomes our unconditional obligation to do whatever promotes our lives and the lives of others and makes it possible for us to live together. Norms of which we can only say that they have proved their worth then acquire unconditional authority.

Such experiences, in which we encounter being itself as a value, take many forms. We often experience reality as so overwhelmingly ordered, so amazingly beautiful, or so vital that we feel an obligation to preserve its order, to build on its beauty, to express its dynamism in our own vitality. All of these experiences are examples of resonance. The order of the world is reflected in our intelligence, the dynamism of nature in our own vitality, the "you" of others in our own "I"—each time we experience something that is undoubtedly objective. But we do not simply observe that this is how things *are* and not otherwise; we immediately affirm that this is how things *must be* and not otherwise. This "must" is not inherent in the objects; it arises from interaction between ourselves and these objects. And this interaction can be described as the experience of a correlation between our selves and reality that allows us to see reality as precious. Experiences of resonance are experiences of value. In them we transcend the world of objects, experiencing in and through the objects a higher value in which the imperative is grounded. Even these experiences can be trivialized. It is possible to say that in such experiences we have imposed on reality imperatives by which we agree to be guided, and the imperative quality of reality rests on a projection of our needs upon reality. In our lives, however, we reject such trivializations. We denounce injustice out of the conviction that it offends against standards we have not fabricated for ourselves but exist independent of us. We rebel against what we see around us.

Let me emphasize once more that the standards to which we appeal can be ascribed to a process of evolutionary development. But this explains only the diffusion of values and norms, not their normativity. If an ethos that has proved its worth for life and for survival is to be normative, at least one norm must be postulated: life has value. Then from this one fundamental value we can derive imperative force for all provisions that promote and preserve life. But this fundamental imperative—something must exist, or being is better than nonbeing—

is based on an experience that I believe must be called religious: the experience that being and responsibility, reality and value are one. Such experiences of resonance also find expression in the Bible in the language of praise and thanksgiving: "Your steadfast love, O LORD, extends to the heavens, your faithfulness to the clouds. Your righteousness is like the mighty mountains, your judgments are like the great deep; you save humans and animals alike, O LORD. How precious is your steadfast love, O God! All people may take refuge in the shadow of your wings. They feast on the abundance of your house, and you give them drink from the river of your delights. For with you is the fountain of life; in your light we see light" (Ps. 36:5-9). The invocative quality of the world is conjured up as the language of physical objects: "The heavens are telling the glory of God; the firmament proclaims his handiwork. Day to day pours forth speech, and night to night declares knowledge. There is no speech, nor are there words; their voice is not heard; yet their voice goes out through all the earth, and their words to the end of the world" (Ps. 19:1-3).

There are thus three fundamental experiences that open the individual to religion: experiences of transcendence, where our cognitive capacity (together with life as a whole) fails us; experiences of contingency, which arouse our sense of creatureliness; and experiences of resonance, in which we experience absolute value. Even in a secularized society, we must try to be sensitive to such experiences and point out their possibility through theoretical reflection. Such experiences do not constitute religion. They may stay diffuse, without making use of a public religious language that leads to a community and establishes an ongoing personal mind-set. They are like a spring: if they are not contained and given direction, the result is a morass. But what must take place for such experiences (and others) to achieve religious articulation? What brings it to pass that some individuals do not trivialize them? Or that the result is not a religious quagmire? The language of the Bible can help. It lends vivid expression to such experiences. But the development of elemental religious experiences into a religious mind-set is also related to the fact that this language activates an inward religious sense able to turn transitory experiences into enduring educational lessons. I am well aware that the dominant theological tradition of the twentieth century found it passé to speak of such a religious sense. A theology of the creative biblical word viewed it as the entering wedge of a reprehensible paganism. But this religious sense is awakened by the biblical word. Strictly speaking, however, this "word" (the *Logos*) is Christ himself. Twentieth-century theology usually found revelation through the *Logos* antithetical to any theology based on universal human experiences and a religious *a priori*. Was this attitude justified? Have people not always used their religious sense to help shape the biblical word? This brings us to the second premise of the Christian religion: belief in a Redeemer.

Faith in a Redeemer and Secular Experience
To the modern mind, the human side of Christology is readily accessible. To look on Jesus as a charismatic whose innovations brought him into conflict with his contemporaries and resulted in his politically motivated execution—that is easy to articulate, as is another aspect of his "humanity," the witnesses to his life and ministry, which need to be interpreted critically. The problem is that the New Testament has surrounded this earthly figure with a mythological aura, making him the Son of God, who came down from heaven and returned to heaven. His earthly life is just a passing phase of his existence. Can this divinization of Jesus also be made accessible? To do so, I believe, it is necessary to have recourse to a religious sense within us that can see far more than a mere human being in a human individual. To illustrate what I mean by this religious sense, I will use a fictional example, the figure of the *homo paradisicus* produced by modern medical technology.

Let us imagine that, in quest of a fulfilled life, several scientists lead us into a room where a sense of absolute happiness is artificially induced in an individual. This *homo paradisicus* is lying on a bed, unaware of the world around him but connected to all sorts of wires and instruments that generate only pleasant feelings and emotions. Why would we refuse to change places with him? Why do we refuse to accept such a life as authentic and fulfilled?

- This *homo paradisicus* is totally dependent on others. He plays no role in his own fulfilled life. He has no chance to be responsible for his life. He is not free. There awakens within us a need for freedom.
- This *homo paradisicus* lives in an illusory world. As soon as we sense that reality and our consciousness of reality are at odds, we are inevitably impelled to accommodate them, and reality takes absolute precedence.

Illusions are beneficent only as long as we do not see through them. Once that happens, they lose their power to make us happy. With the imperative of truth, there awakens within us a need for the unconditional—for something that takes precedence over our own ideas, even our own lives, under all conditions.

- A third characteristic of our lives cannot be illustrated by this example but only by reflection on it. Once we have concluded that this totally artificial *homo paradisicus* does not enjoy a fulfilled life, we can claim that the truth of this realization is "eternal." For if it is true, it is true for all time—even for seven million + n years. Even quite trivial truths, if true at all, are true forever. If it is true to say that it rained on day x, even in seven million + n years it will be true to say that it rained on day x.

There is latent within us a sense for freedom, for the absolute, and for the eternal—even if we are unaware of it. Of course, we can deliberately deny the setting in which we live. Many deliberately deny human freedom. But for their conviction that humans are not free they claim that their thesis is based on more than physical determinism. In that case, it would be impossible to say, "It is true," but only, "All the factors of our world to date have led to someone's saying this and nothing else." And any contrary thesis would have the same right, for it, too, would be determined. Anyone who utters it could do nothing other than utter it, since it is completely predetermined. Debate about truth would be meaningless.

This need for eternity, absoluteness, and responsibility becomes productive in religion. Using snapshots of the world we live in, it constructs images that far transcend this world. I assume that it is this very need for freedom, the unconditional, and the eternal that is activated when people study the symbolic world of religion. Although there is no *a priori* human knowledge of God, there are preconditions without which we would never arrive at an understanding of God. For the "unconditional" and "eternal" is not identical with the living God. God is more than that. And a sense for freedom and responsibility can also be developed without an awareness of God. And yet, without a sense for the unconditional, the eternal, and responsibility we would have no access to the idea of God in the biblical texts. Let me describe briefly how religious categories are activated by fundamental religious experiences:

1. Experiences of transcendence can activate a sense for the unconditional. We are driven by an imperative to sacrifice all our errors and illusions (associated with the limited world in which we live) on the altar of reality. If we say we would rather have a beneficial illusion than the truth, then we give what is beneficial precedence over truth. Here we always follow our sense for the unconditional, which inevitably brings us to prefer what is normatively superior to what is normatively inferior. And we do so even when we know that this objective is unreachable. For we shall never be able to transcend the constructs of our own thought and reason so as to look reality per se in the eye. Nevertheless, a sense for the unconditional drives us to seek an unconditional, absolute truth transcending the empirical world.

2. If we do not trivialize experiences of contingency but accept our own feeling of creatureliness, this feeling rests on a confrontation with the nothingness from which we come and into which we shall vanish. This nothingness is unending. Once we have entered it, it never ceases. But for this very reason, it evokes a sense for what is eternal. We understand involuntarily that the nothingness that swallows us up is eternal. And we are aware at the same time that our transitory existence is recorded forever in the book of being, even when we have entered the black hole of nothingness. In $x + n$ years, it will still be true that we existed. In $x + n$ years, it will still be true that today we thought about what will be true in $x + n$ years. Thus, confrontation with nothingness awakens in us a sense for the eternal: both limitless nothingness and the eternal truth of a passing moment.

3. If we do not dismiss experiences of resonance as suggestions but treat them as imperatives that help us live authentically, it is because they activate a sense for freedom—a responsibility for our lives that no one can take from us. Let me once again use an example to illustrate the demands made by such experiences of resonance: A friend has a holiday and goes to the Alps to relax. First of all, the Alpine scenery is a means to an end. He hopes that it will be a good place for him to unwind and regain strength. But as he stands on his skis and looks out over the virgin snow, he feels an urge not to make any old curve with his skis, but to make a beautiful curve, the fascinating line of which will do justice to the countryside. We experience the same imperative in our lives. We set out into the world and expect that it will meet our

needs. But then we are seized by a mission in this world that comes to us like a call. It is not the world that is at our service; we are instead in the service of a cause, as though it were our responsibility to continue the history of this world in a way that makes sense. To an objectified worldview, such experiences are a "soft" domain of reality: the world of men and women, their decisions, plans, dreams, morality. But this reality is where the authentic lives of human beings are lived. We may leave unanswered the question of what we really are—whether we are ruled by our drives or govern our lives rationally—but it is in this "blank" within reality, waiting to be filled in, that our lives are realized.

We can say in summary that the elemental religious experiences of transcendence, contingency, and resonance awaken in us a "self" that is aware of its own unmistakable significance. It is in contact with the unconditional and eternal, and it is realized in its own unique responsibility. It has its life as a mission that can be shirked or fulfilled. It seeks what it truly is and what is still undecided. And here the Bible can play a decisive role. Its texts are often quite strange—legendary, whimsical, fictitious. But they work on us and in us, because they speak to something latent within us: they confront us with a call to responsibility, a call that possesses the unconditional nature of the holy and establishes contact with an eternal reality. Religion arises from this confluence of fundamental existential experiences and the categories of the religious sense within us, but always mediated by a concrete, traditional symbolic language of religion like that found in the Bible. Now we can formulate an answer to the questions, Why do we read the Bible? And why do we teach it? The most important purpose is instruction in a religious language that can—but need not—become the language of vital religious experience. But why the Bible in particular? Why not some other book? The first answer has to do with its content.

In the New Testament, the focal point of this religious language is Jesus Christ—both a human individual and the Redeemer. And here, I believe, it is unmistakable that a sense for the eternal, the unconditional, and responsibility has contributed to the picture of this figure. A transitory phenomenon, living under specific conditions, unmistakably determined by social and political factors, was recognized as the manifestation of an eternal and unconditional figure, demanding our responsibility. There-fore, this figure came to be surrounded poetically by the mythic aura appropriate to a divine being. But the aura did not displace the original figure. The memory was preserved that Jesus was also mortal, contingent, and constrained—in other words, a concrete historical figure. Did not the inner persuasiveness of his image for the first Christians rest on the fact that Christology was consonant with the structure of the human self, a human self with a sense for the eternal, the unconditional, and freedom, yet vulnerable to mortality, contingency, and constraint? Could Jesus occupy this central position in the newborn Christian religion because he awakened the human religious sense and reconciled it with everyday earthly reality? We saw that in the New Testament all the fundamental motifs are associated with the figure of Jesus Christ. His image in the New Testament is like the incarnation of these motifs. To understand the fig-ure of Christ, it is therefore crucial to discover secular analogies to these fundamental motifs, to make them plausible to outsiders.

Secular Points of Entry for the Core Themes of the Bible
Corresponding to the fundamental biblical motifs, the secular conscious-ness provides convergent or alternative motifs. These will often raise the question whether they represent secularized biblical traditions or inde-pendent analogies produced by encounters with the same reality. In the discussion that follows, I shall first point descriptively to such "secular" analogies; then in a second section I shall add a theoretical interpretation that not everyone will necessarily share: an evolutionary interpretation of the fundamental motifs of biblical religion. It may serve to represent attempts to express the issues of the biblical faith in modern language. But in principle other interpretations are also possible.

Creation. Awareness of the contingency of all things is the counterpart to the creation motif. The Greeks and Romans did not have an awareness of the irrational contingency of the existence of all things as pervasive as that of Jews and Christians, whose eyes were opened to this contin-gency by the biblical belief in creation. It traces the very being of things to an unaccountable command of God. In the course of Western history, however, this awareness of contingency has drifted away from its pos-sible context of discovery. Today it is closely associated with empirical science, which is convinced *a priori* that we do not attain knowledge of reality through logical deduction but only through confrontation with facts and data that no thought process can anticipate. The quiddity and quality of the world are contingent. They cannot be deduced *a priori* but only observed *a posteriori*.

In an evolutionary framework, the biblical creation motif, like the secular motif of contingency, is an expression of the irrational process that brings forth an extravagant variety of forms of life and being, only a few of which survive. Evolution takes place through the interplay of "chance and necessity." Chance is allied with contingency, creativity, novelty, unpredictability. It manifests itself in the mutations of biological evolution, in the recombination of elements. It does not involve *creatio ex nihilo*, but it does involve creation through new structures and combinations that never were. Of all these innovations, natural selection preserves whatever has a chance for survival because it is consonant with the fundamental conditions of reality. Most mutations perish because they are not sufficiently adapted to the environment and the architecture of the organism to provide an advantage. This interplay of chance and necessity, of creation and survival, is profoundly transformed in one critical aspect by the New Testament: what is "unfit" and "lost" is saved by God's creative power—the very things marked for destruction by natural selection. The crucified Jesus had been rejected; he was to vanish from the stage of history, the weakling whose impotence was vividly demonstrated. But to this very Jesus God gave new life. In the resurrection of Jesus from the dead, God's creative power interrupts the course of history with an anti-selectionist protest.

Wisdom. The counterpart to the wisdom motif is the regularity of the world postulated by all the sciences. It is axiomatic to every scientific experiment and theory. Nevertheless, this trust in the world's orderliness is the product of historical development. In five hundred years of intensive engagement with the natural sciences, we have gained a constantly improving picture of the laws and regularities governing nature, although there is no necessary reason for this order. Reality could have been different, even though complex structures like human beings would hardly stand a chance in a less orderly world. We can only observe that the world is surprisingly orderly and that its fundamental structures make life possible (the anthropic principle).

Within an evolutionary framework, the wisdom motif discloses the consonance between creation and human life. The structures of the created world are supportive of life; those who are guided by them will live. In the biblical worldview, this "fit" between the world and humankind is an accompaniment of creation; to evolutionary thought, it is the result of a long process of adaptation. The New Testament reflects a crisis of this adaptive process: wisdom turns into folly. What is totally "maladapted" is more consonant with ultimate reality than what seems to be "strong" and successful.

Miracle. In the modern world, the counterpart to the miracle motif is a strong indeterminism: trust in chance and the knowledge that the course of history is not set in stone. Here the modern mind is divided. It is natural for us to vacillate between determinism and a sense of freedom. Leaving aside such theoretical convictions, however, in our immediate everyday consciousness we all spontaneously lay claim to freedom and responsibility—otherwise blame and commitment would be absurd. And likewise in our meta-reflection on our theories of determinism or indeterminism we all lay claim to freedom, for these theories would undermine themselves if determinism were applied to their origin.

Where can an evolutionary interpretation begin? Miracles intervene where life would otherwise be without hope: among the starving, the imperiled, the sick, the dying. We may sometimes be irritated by the bizarre miracles of the Gospels, but they simply and forcefully express the anti-selectionist protest that informs the entire Bible.

Alienation. There are many motifs in today's secular culture that converge with the motif of alienation. We find a profound sense of absurdity, which can reach the extreme of modern self-loathing. Such experiences signal a deep alienation from ourselves. And this sense of alienation has not lessened with the liberalization of norms and lifestyles. Indeed, it is even more oppressive when self-chosen norms and lifestyles fail than in the case of the traditional norms of society. Here the cause of the failure lies within us. And the damage goes deep.

In an evolutionary interpretation, a sense of alienation illuminates incongruities between human beings and creation. Despite all the structures of adaptation, we experience ourselves as "maladapted," both to the everyday world and to ultimate reality. We miss life's promise, which should consist in total congruity with reality. Sin and suffering demonstrate our alienation from this perfect state. They represent evolutionary pain, the "groaning of creation" for a new world.

Hope, Exodus, and Conversion. The counterpart to the motif of renewal is a utopian sensibility that insists on transforming the world. All of modern history resounds with such utopias, for good or ill. The exodus ever and again reappears transformed in the diverse liberation movements of the modern age, seeking liberation for workers, for youth, for women. On the level of the individual, the counterpart to the motif of renewal is a therapeutic culture that believes it is possible to change conduct for the better. Sometimes change is even embraced with enthusiasm. At the very least, the various schools of therapy share the belief that the way we deal with the condition of our lives can be changed constructively.

The motif of renewal enshrines an evolutionary sense of passage. In Daniel's vision (Daniel 7), the sequence of kingdoms is seen as a passage from the dominion of "beasts" to the dominion of "one like a human being." In early Christianity, Jesus became this figure. The new kingdom bears his sign, not that of the beasts. Does this not mark the first glimmer of an awareness that we are passing from biological to cultural evolution? That we, in the midst of history, are still in transition from bestiality to humanity? And does this awareness not contain a germ of truth?

Indwelling. The counterpart to the motif of dwelling is the modern insistence that everything spiritual should take sensible, corporeal form. We live in a culture that glorifies the body and the senses, possibly because we often do violence to our bodies and senses through excessive workplace discipline. The longing for corporeality repeatedly makes itself felt: thought finds embodiment in the cult of nonverbal communication, abstract life in the cult of sport. In the din of the "Love Parade," the cult of the body is commercialized.

The motif of dwelling pictures the human individual as a "blank" to be filled with a new being and transformed by the spirit of God. Through rebirth, the individual can acquire "organs" sensitive to a deeper reality that transcends the everyday world and gives assurance that the law of the jungle is only the perspective of the limited world we inhabit. Christ is the prototype of the individual so transformed, who gives access to a world of peace and reconciliation. The incarnation of God in Christ is comparable to a creative "mutation" that suddenly enhances the "adaptation" of humanity to ultimate reality and gives access to new dimensions.

Substitution. The motif of substitution or of vicarious representation can connect with the modern awareness that living creatures share one stream of life. This awareness can even draw on naturalistic evidence. Something of us lives in all living creatures. Our genetic code is remarkably similar even to that of insects. Awareness that human beings are not interchangeable emerges only with the sense of personal individuality. Our material bodies, however—our corporeality—connect us with the natural world. And this connection can be experienced in a cosmic sense of connection. If I am dust and ashes, I can recognize myself in dust and ashes. If I am flesh and blood, I can vicariously experience all flesh and blood as being related to me. Vegetarianism rebels against our harsh treatment of other living creatures.

From the evolutionary perspective, the motif of substitution is twofold: it both embodies and protests the principle of natural selection. On the one hand, all life lives at the expense of other life. Unfit life dies vicariously for the life of ascendant creatures. In this sense, vicarious representation is an expression of natural selection. Those who compete in the "struggle for life" make others pay the cost of their survival. On the other hand, the christological symbolism of vicarious death turns this perspective upside down. Here life does not live at the expense of other life but accepts death willingly to make life possible. Above all, however, the life that is sacrificed does not remain in the thrall of death. It overcomes death and thus nullifies the law that life must live at the expense of other life.

Faith. The motif of faith has its counterpart in a humanistic "culture of interaction" and an awareness that basic trust is fundamentally important for all of life. Relationships with the first significant persons in our lives are the key to establishing this basic trust. It is well known that no one acquires this trust in isolation: it is always an echo of trust that is given.

The motif of faith reflects our experience that without trust we run aground in the stream of events (both historical and evolutionary). This trust is based on encounters with others, in which take place those "qualitative leaps" that enable and promise a greater congruence with ultimate reality. All in whom the spirit manifests its transforming power can renew faith. In the New Testament, Jesus stands at the center of this constant establishment and renewal of faith: he is the "pioneer of our faith" (Heb. 12:2).

Love (*Agapē*). The secular counterpart of the *agapē* motif is a solidarity that deliberately includes aliens and strangers. Love of neighbor has become a universal value, even if in our modern society we pursue very different ethical programs that are at odds with it. A program of power aims to master and prevail, while a contrarian program aims to befriend and help. Relief organizations spring up everywhere. We invest enormous quantities of time and money in establishing and maintaining them.

The *agapē* motif suggests the passage from biological to cultural evolution. In biological evolution, success goes to the combination of love toward one's genetic kin and aggression toward others. Early Christianity turned this combination on its head. It required love toward enemies, strangers, and sinners and aggression toward one's genetic kin, bluntly demanding Jesus' followers to forsake father and family.

Status Reversal. The motif of reversal of status is alive and well in the antiauthoritarian mood of the modern world. Whoever is on top must be ready to accept the role of all the rest; whoever would rule must also know how to serve. In the modern world, even extreme self-abasement in the form of self-stigmatization can be a creative strategy for change: we see it in the techniques used in actions and demonstrations.

In an evolutionary framework, we can locate the motif of change of status in that borderline situation between biological and cultural evolution that characterizes human life: in animal societies, hierarchy and pecking order clearly contribute to survival. The most powerful animals are favored because they are important to the group for defense against attack from without and for coordination within. But if the first is the one who adopts the position of the last, this basic principle of biological evolution is invalidated.

Judgment. The motif of judgment finds an echo in awareness of personal responsibility—if not to God, at least to our own conscience. It is true that now and again people rebel against turning life into a "tribunal." In reality, however, we are constantly seeking to justify ourselves: our own conduct, our society, the entire world. The expectation of God's judgment even seems at times to be more merciful than human self-judgment, which internalizes judgment day. But the secular mentality also provides a counterpoise: belief in the justification of sinners has its counterpart in belief in the ineradicable dignity of the individual—regardless of deeds and transgressions.

An evolutionary interpretation of the judgment motif is almost inescapable. All life is lived under the harsh pressure of natural selection, which distinguishes those forms of life and behavior that are fit from those that are not. This objective pressure of selection manifests itself in fantasies of the last judgment: only those who meet the new world's criteria may enter it. And in New Testament texts, they are precisely those excluded by natural selection: the weak and unfit. The godless are justified by God's judgment. The gospel of the sinner's acquittal abrogates the pressure of selection and embodies an anti-Darwinian protest.

These reflections have attempted to show that the symbolic language of the Bible, which continues to fascinate many while alienating others because of the archaic and mythological features of its contents, finds analogous counterparts to its themes and fundamental motifs in the secular mentality of our present-day culture. Even those who do not wish to adopt the symbolic language of the Bible as their own can, with its help, better understand those who do. This insight alone provides an important reason for promoting an increased public biblical literacy, in both educational systems and our general culture. For this dialogue with the secular world, we need a philosophy of religion that is free of confessional interests. Many questions that theologians have long dismissed as outmoded apologetics or "natural theology" take on great importance in real life. The discourse of theologians often breathes an atmosphere in which such questions are hardly open to discussion. Elemental discussions about God are quickly dismissed as "confirmation class questions" (I speak from experience). Perhaps this speaks more for the young people who ask them than for the theologians who think they have outgrown them!

The goal of dialogue with the secular world is to enable a religious understanding of reality. We recall once more that belief in a preexisting meaning of reality is the defining characteristic of religion. Such belief cannot be demonstrated, but it can be experienced as being "spoken to" from without, both in the self-disclosure of an existing meaning and in the aspiration to realize that meaning in one's own life. The preexistence of this meaning and aspiration is guaranteed by an authority that is more than human (even if it appears only as a total system of reality). The conundrum is how we can shift from a secular to a religious interpretation of reality—and how we can enable others, particularly the young, to make this perceptual shift.

This shift is comparable to the way we look at figure/ground illusions. We are all familiar with such images, which Gestalt psychologists use to show that perception is an active process. When we reverse figure and ground, we see first a chalice, then two faces in profile; first an old woman, then a young woman; first a glass half empty, then a glass half full. In each case we perform a cognitive restructuring of our perception, which itself remains objectively unchanged. Reality itself remains unchanged when perceived religiously, but it is restructured on the basis of an inner "search program." The convictions and motifs of religions constitute such a program: they create a preconception in light of which we see and experience reality differently than when we view it from a secular perspective. Scandinavian psychology of religion ascribes the alternation between secular and religious perception to such conceptual restructuring, based above all on role models we follow in adapting to reality.

The role the Bible may play in this process can be illustrated by the parable of the laborers in the vineyard (Matt. 20:11-16). If we disregard the introductory metaphor formula, the parable can be read as a secular story about the workaday world. It does not explicitly mention God. Once a student prepared a sermon about Matthew 20:1-16 that was rejected because it did not contain the word *God*—even though its failure to mention God did not reflect a "theology after the death of God." The sermon had simply followed the narrative dynamic of the parable and was content to contrast justice and mercy. Where might the preacher (likewise without using the metaphor formula) have suggested that this parable makes the everyday world transparent to something "wholly other"? Clearly, at the point where the story's "extravagance" shatters normal expectations: when all the laborers receive the same pay regardless of how long they worked. No earthly employer acts like that! A reader alerted by the introductory formula would suspect all along that the employer represents God; now, however, God appears clearly—and acts not like an employer but like a father. It would therefore be a mistake to reject totally the "secular" interpretation of the student described above. If this God acts quite unlike an employer, that is an indirect criticism of real employers in Jesus' day. What brings the parable to life is its contrast with actual behavior.

But this reading does not exhaust the restructuring impulse of the parable. The point is that what we perceive as "outrageous" is an expression of sovereign "generosity." It is outrageous not just in the workaday world but in reality as a whole that human conduct is not "rewarded." Bad things often happen to good people, and the wicked often prosper amazingly. This ethical irrationality of the world is a challenge to the religious perception of reality. In the parables and sayings of Jesus, we find occasion to reinterpret even such repugnant experiences, making them a motivation for faith and a spur to action. We may consider identical reward for different conduct to be an injustice to the good, but also to be merciful generosity shown the "others." Then the ethical irrationality of the world becomes a sign of God's mercy, giving the wicked a chance. The most impressive restructuring of this sort is in the exhortation to love our enemies. That the sun rises indifferently on both the good and evil should actually lead to resigned acceptance. Ecclesiastes uses the image of the sun in this sense. The Jesus tradition, however, restructures this pessimistic picture positively: God manifests divine grace by making the sun rise on the evil and on the good. We should follow God's example, treating both the good and evil magnanimously.

The Bible is full of stories and texts that enable secular perceptions to be restructured religiously. We find analogous texts in all religions. The Bible is one book among many competing sacred books. Why should we assign it a privileged place? Just as important as dialogue with the secular world-view, therefore, is the ability to enter into dialogue with other religions.

THE BIBLE IN DIALOGUE WITH OTHER RELIGIONS

Western culture is often charged with having lost its sense of the sacred, of living in an "eclipse of God." The more Western civilization appears superior, the more other religions make this accusation. Today dialogue with these religions is no longer dialogue with other lands and cultures, but dialogue at home: there are many Muslims among us, and small groups are devotees of Eastern religions. Interfaith dialogue has become a necessity for inward and outward peace. Any study of religion or the Bible must deal with it—the more so because we share the Old Testament with Judaism, and Islam fundamentally respects and honors the Bible.

We must work with the Bible in a context of dialogue, from one of three classic positions:

1. *Exclusivism* supports the sole truth of one single religion and denies the truth of all others. Religions are either characterized as "law," demanding salvation through one's own efforts in contrast to the gospel, or as human artifacts in contrast to God's revelation.
2. *Inclusivism* admits the truth of other religions, but only insofar as it is realized in one's own religion. This position pervades Catholic theology and often makes it more open to religious dialogue than many schools of Protestant theology.
3. *Pluralism* teaches the equality of all religions, either because they all relate to the mysterious ultimate reality, or because they all seek human salvation. Some small groups of modern theologians espouse this position.

A fourth position, *dialogism*, might be added. It makes no final judgments about other religions but seeks only to define the way in which interfaith dialogue can take place—namely according to rules embodying two elements: respect and appreciation for other religions and authentic advocacy of one's own cause. Pluralism reflects our pluralistic situation. But it is often inclusivism in disguise—not from the standpoint of an existing religion, but from that of a hypothetical religious synthesis that seeks to combine the elements of truth found in all religions. From this perspective of superiority, it looks down on all religions; by expecting them to relativize their own claims, it asks too much of them.

Dialogism reflects the limits of our finite knowledge, but runs the risk of abandoning prematurely attempts to penetrate the multiplicity of religions theoretically and scrutinize them to identify their truth.

I believe that there are four ways we can use the Bible to support interfaith dialogue: by interpreting texts, by tracing their origin, by examining their influence, and by comparing them with other texts. We interpret biblical texts that refer to other religions, we identify within the Bible echoes of other religions, we study the influence of the Bible within other religions, or we compare biblical texts with the scriptures of other religions, without positing a historical connection between the Bible and those texts.

On the level of textual interpretation, we encounter people of many religions in the Bible. The primal history addresses all nations, not just Israel. The election of Israel is set in a universalist context. On the one hand, it is instrumental, enabling the fulfillment of God's commandments and the attestation of God's existence to the world. On the other, it is a value in and of itself, inasmuch as God in his unfathomable love chose this one nation and no other. Biblical wisdom enshrines universally accessible knowledge. Job, the paradigmatic upright man of the Old Testament, lived in "the land of Uz"; he was not a Jew. The future hope of the Old Testament is also universalistic: prophecy looks for all nations to affirm the one and only God. The prophets' criticism of Israel's religious egoism and the short book of Jonah show that within Israel universalist ideas could protest against particularism: the reaction of Gentile Nineveh was exemplary, that of the Jewish prophet narrow-minded. In the New Testament, the breakdown of the boundary between Israel and other nations is foreshadowed in Jesus; in early Christianity it becomes programmatic. Paul opens Christianity to all nations. At the same time, however, we find a twofold absolutism: in the Old Testament, the monotheistic demand of God for exclusive worship (Exod. 20:2-3); in the New, the absolute claim of Christology, whether in the words of the Johannine Jesus, "I am the way, and the truth, and the life. No one comes to the Father except through me" (John 14:6), or in the words of Peter, "There is salvation in no one else, for there is no other name under heaven given among mortals by which we must be saved" (Acts 4:12). Interfaith learning using the Bible must not ignore such awkward texts, but rather expand and develop them. According to the First Commandment in the Decalogue, the one and only God is the God who led Egypt out of bondage. Here freedom is held up as an absolute value. The Johannine Jesus champions the way of love.[2] The goal of his absolute claim is love. The Christ of Luke and Acts demands repentance and conversion. The goal of his absolute claim is conversion. Of course, such interpretations treat the biblical text freely, but they develop it responsibly.

A genetic reading of biblical texts can deepen their interfaith dimension—above and beyond texts that describe encounters with people of other religions. In fact, the anti-syncretistic self-image of biblical religion—that is, its presumed opposition to the blending of belief systems—lives in tension with its borrowing of many ideas and motifs from other religions. For instance, a wealth of parallels to the biblical creation account may be found in the scriptures of other religions. The Proverbs of Solomon incorporate portions of the Wisdom of Amen-em-ope (Prov. 22:17—23:11; 24:10-12). In the psalter we hear echoes of prayers from the entire ancient Near East. The religio-historical school has taught us to search the Bible for disguised source texts and parallels from other religions. Even if many proposed borrowings and analogies are outdated, it remains true that in the Bible we hear the voices of many religions. This approach, of course, takes us only to the religions of the ancient world, for only they could leave direct or indirect traces in biblical texts.

Study of the Bible's influence also includes more modern religions in which the Bible has left traces. Jews share the Old Testament with Christians and have had to distinguish themselves from Christians. Muhammad referred to Abraham and Jesus. He ascribed revelatory character to the Bible and understood himself to be the Paraclete promised in the Gospel of John. The Bible has influenced many texts in Islam. When we examine Judaism, Christianity, and Islam, we see that a later religion often preserves possibilities inherent in an earlier religion that would otherwise have perished. In the New Testament, Jews find a fragment of their own history that they are beginning to reappropriate: the history of a Jewish renewal movement that Judaism rejected. In the Jesus of the Qur'an, Christians today encounter a Jesus who vanished with Jewish Christianity: a theocentric prophet who focused not on himself but on the one and only God. Beyond all doubt: the three Western religions of Judaism, Christianity, and Islam are intimately connected from the start. Their contact with Eastern religions has been secondary. Only in the modern period has the Bible influenced Hindus and Buddhists. But here, too, the encounter has disclosed possibilities that had been buried in the Western tradition, as the example of Mahatma Gandhi illustrates.

A functional comparison of two religions is possible apart from any influence or genetic relationship. All religions deal with comparable problems, structures, and forms of expression. The phenomenology of religion has described them and constructed typologies of religions to display their variety. Especially where there has been no substantial contact between two religions until the modern period, functional comparison is reasonable. Even if typologies represent fictional ideals, we cannot do without them as ways of ordering the material. Only a precise definition of the diverse structures of religion can assign Christianity its special place: among all Western religions, it most closely resembles Eastern religions. We will show that in many respects it occupies a middle ground—which implies not privilege but responsibility.

In interfaith dialogue, too, we investigate the fundamental motifs of other religions and not their "letter." Christians have many motifs in common with Jews and Muslims: creation, wisdom, miracles, renewal, faith, *agapē*, and judgment. Dialogue with the mystical religions of the East appears more difficult. But there, too, we should look behind the differences to identify deeper similarities. At the same time, we must reckon with the possibility that even on a deeper level the Eastern religions are shaped by core convictions and motifs different from those of the West. But behind the intricate network of differing basic convictions, we may still discover similarities that might be significant for the self-image of both.

Debate with other religions helps make the profile of each religion clearer. For an outsider, comparison of religions is a good introduction to an understanding of religion in general. For the adherents of a particular religion, it can aid deeper insight into their own tradition so that they become better Christians, better Muslims, or better Buddhists—and can gauge the limits of their own religion.

Religious Typologies as an Attempt for an Overview of Religions
No religion can observe other religions from a perspective outside our world, although we have toyed with this idea in the fiction of an inter-planetary study of religion. But even from our own finite perspective,

we can employ criteria to distinguish them. All religious typologies are biased, but use of different typologies simultaneously can eliminate many biases. Here we outline five, beginning with the distinction between primary religions and scriptural religions. Within scriptural religions, there follow the distinctions between prophetic and mystical religions, anthropocentric and theocentric religions, between national religions and universal religions, religions of reconciliation and religions of redemption. The first distinction is fundamental, because all religions have in common a primary religious stratum, which is both expanded and criticized in the scriptural religion.

1. Primary Religions and Scriptural Religions. The religions of preliterate cultures have often been distinguished from the world religions by such pejorative descriptions as "primitive." This distinction itself is biased, because nonscriptural religions live on in scriptural religions. Scriptural religions arose through criticism of existing religious practice. Not only do they presuppose the discovery of writing (as a necessary condition for departing from ancestral traditions and replacing them with other "canonical" memories), they also record their insights in writing. But in doing so they base themselves on the forms of expression used by the "primitive religions." It is therefore more appropriate to call the religions of preliterate peoples "primary religions." They characteristically sanctify the world and human existence. They legitimate the fact that the world and humanity are as they are and assign humanity a home within this world. This process begins with the religious interpretation of the genealogical community, the foundation of life. Time is sanctified as the power that imposes order on life, manifesting itself in the cycles of days, moons, and years, and in the course of human life. Space and the Earth are sanctified because they make life possible. Sacred times and sacred spaces make it possible to celebrate festivals that surround life with a numinous glow. The same is true of the arrangements governing society. They constitute a natural order, which could not be conceived otherwise than it is. Deities are concretely related to the sensible world: springs and mountains, rain and tempests, fertility and war. Their transcendence is limited.

The appearance of scriptural religions is always associated with religious criticism of this sanctification of the world by primary religions.

This criticism is incorporated into the sacred texts of these religions (and inspires their theologians), while everyday life perpetuates primary religious traditions. The understanding of God is criticized: the polytheism of pagans is sharply rejected in the monotheistic religions, and Islam even criticizes the Christian Trinity as a reversion to outdated paganism. The image of God becomes increasingly transcendent. Only at this point does religion become something "wholly other," in contrast to this world. Therefore, all-too-earthly representations of the Deity are criticized—above all in Judaism, Islam, and the iconoclastic traditions of Christianity. In the context of the cult, reliance on sacrifice coupled with neglect of justice is criticized by the prophets—as the inability of sacrifice to redeem humankind is criticized in the religions of India, the Upanishads, Buddhism, and Jainism. The religious veil is stripped from the existing world in vehement criticism that foresees its destruction: both Jesus and Muhammad proclaimed the imminent end of this world. It is not as it should be, and therefore judgment awaits it. Without such apocalyptic expectations, Indian religions also view the world from a negative and critical perspective—a view that culminates in Buddhism, which realizes that this world is a prison and conceives of redemption as its dissolution. Finally, the existing laws governing life are criticized: the Torah is criticized in Christianity, the traditional laws of Arabia in Islam. Above all, however, all religions give birth to breakaway movements, itinerant monks and ascetics. And naturally the self-assurance of primary religions is challenged by splinter groups. John the Baptist is simply voicing such criticism when he warns the Jews not to feel secure just because they are descended from Abraham. All scriptural religions therefore embody criticism of religion. Here they differ from primary religious, which survive within them as a fundamental stratum of religious experience and behavior. As a religion critical of religion, Christianity is only one religion among others. Then how can it be distinguished within the group of scriptural religions critical of religion? What are its unique features? Here other typologies of religion come to our aid.

2. Prophetic Religions and Mystical Religions. Prophetic religions and mystical religions are responses to uncertainty with regard to the basic premise of all religions: that reality has meaning. This meaning is no longer a given, but must be discovered or realized. The urgent question also surfaces in intersecular dialogue: Does reality in fact have a preexistent meaning that we can embrace in our lives? Or do we ourselves impose this meaning on the world? Since the sensible world often appears to be empty of meaning, all religions are aware of the difference between the phenomenal world and reality per se. Only contact with reality per se gives us confidence that we are responding to values that we ourselves did not create and obeying imperatives that we ourselves did not formulate! Here religious experience opens two possibilities: We may come in contact with ultimate reality when confronted with it by a "call" from without. That is the way of prophetic religions. In them charismatics confront those around them with irruptions of ultimate reality, bringing a message from outside the world of everyday experience. But we can also approach ultimate reality on the "inner way." Behind our experience and perception of ourselves, we are part of or creatures of reality per se. That is the way of mystical religions. They seek enlightenment that discloses ultimate reality as our own proper "home." The goal of mystical religions is not confrontation with the "wholly other," which comes to us from without, but union with the "wholly near," from which we are separated. These two fundamental possibilities for religious thought and experience constantly resurface. In all prophetic religions, we find mystical strands such as Jewish Hasidism, Christian mysticism, and Islamic Sufism. In mystical religion, conversely, we repeatedly encounter prophetic movements. Interfaith encounters help us rediscover and appreciate some of our own forgotten traditions: the mystical religions of the East, for example, remind us of the mysticism of early Christianity and the Middle Ages. Even though Christianity is by and large a prophetic religion, it has repeatedly been interpreted "mystically." Jesus is the Word of God, who speaks to us and galvanizes us from without, but this Word can be embodied in every Christian. Therefore, there is a legitimate Christ mysticism in the New Testament—a mysticism of Word, will, and community.

A more consistent mysticism appeared in early Christianity shortly after the New Testament. Its most impressive document is the *Gospel of Thomas*, which was not included in the canon. Perhaps it was not even excluded deliberately, for it and other Thomas traditions originated in eastern Syria, an area far removed from the formation of the canon. Even if it had been known in Rome and Asia Minor, the centers of "canonical" Christianity, its acceptance would have faced difficulties because of its radical individualism and its Gnostic tinge. In the *Gospel of Thomas*, Jesus' message of the kingdom of God becomes a message of the discovery of the true self: all people are lost sparks from the divine world; Jesus reminds them of their heavenly home and through his call they discover the infinite value at the center of their own lives. The text begins with a promise to its readers that they will advance to eternal life if they find the concealed significance of Jesus' words, their mystic interpretation (*Gos. Thom.* 1). They must seek it and not be led astray in their search. They will find the Archimedean point—that is, the independent vantage point—from which they can reign over all. This Archimedean point is the inner self (*Gos. Thom.* 2). The next saying interprets the reign of God programmatically as the inner self, quite in keeping with Jesus' words in Luke 17:21: "Jesus said, If your leaders say to you, 'Look, the kingdom is in the sky,' then the birds of the sky will precede you. If they say to you, 'It is in the sea,' then the fish will precede you. Rather, the kingdom is within you and it is outside you. When you know yourselves, then you will be known, and you will understand that you are children of the living Father. But if you do not know yourselves, then you live in poverty, and you are poverty" (*Gos. Thom.* 3).

There is no room here for a full discussion of this collection and interpretation of Jesus' words. One thing does need to be emphasized, however: it does not share the features that led to the rejection of Gnosticism. There is no trace of a demiurge in addition to God, nor does it embody a docetic Christology that denies the incarnation. In any case it is well suited for building a bridge to the Eastern religions, for its aim is the intuitive insight that the inner self is identical with the reign of God. This insight derives in part from a reinterpretation of the traditional sayings of Jesus in the Synoptic Gospels, and in part from previously unknown sayings of Jesus (in large measure fresh coinages in the spirit of this mystical piety). Such traditions, in part suppressed and in part lost, should be heard when the Bible is taught today, to illustrate the range of early Christianity. It may be by accident that now and again one of the sayings of Jesus in the *Gospel of Thomas* has been preserved in other religions. For example, we read, "Jesus said, Become passers-by" (*Gos. Thom.* 42). This recalls an Arabic inscription from the ruins of Fatehpur Sikri, a city in northern India, which says: "The world is a bridge. Pass over it, but do not settle on it."

3. Anthropocentric Religions and Theocentric Religions. These two ways of establishing contact with ultimate reality give rise to theocentric and anthropocentric religions. At the center of mystical religions is the human person and enlightenment; at the center of prophetic religions is God. Christianity is one of the Western religions, but it is neither purely theocentric nor anthropocentric. It is christocentric. Its core is belief in God's real presence in a human individual—as a prototype showing that God seeks to be present through God's spirit in each individual. The individual is possessed by God's spirit, which shapes and transforms the human will. The way of the spirit does not lead inward to hidden depths of the self, but forward: the individual becomes a new creation.

4. National Religions and Universal Religions. Judaism and Hinduism are tied to individual nations. The religion of postexilic Israel made it a nation with an ongoing identity. Hinduism, however, embraces many religions and peoples, but it was only their common self-identification distinct from the Muslims and British that made them a nation. It is in this sense that Hinduism can be categorized as a national religion. Other religions such as Buddhism and Christianity attract adherents from many nations. They are missionary religions. These two types of religion—national and universal—embody different understandings of salvation. In a national religion, the individual is born into a positive state of salvation; what matters is to preserve it. In universal religions, by contrast, salvation does not rest in an initial status but in a new status that must be found. Human beings are in need of redemption and must change. Judaism is a national religion, even though it has universalistic features: it awaits worldwide recognition of the one and only God. Christianity adopts these universalistic tendencies of Judaism and constructs a universal missionary religion. At this point it develops a pessimistic anthropology, which we encounter in Paul, the missionary to the Gentiles. According to Paul, people can be saved only through a profound transformation. They must die with Christ and enter into a new life. Buddhism is a universal religion that emerged within Hinduism. In Buddhism, too, we can observe this intensely pessimistic anthropology. The human self is an illusion from which the individual must be set free.

Here, too, early Christianity stood at a threshold, having to decide if it would remain bound to a national religion. Did one have to become a Jew in order to become a Christian? This would have meant accepting the marks of Jewish identity: circumcision and the dietary laws. Others, such as Paul, wanted to open the new faith to all peoples and nations. Accordingly, we have two anthropologies in the New Testament. Where Judaism is stronger, we find an optimistic anthropology: the Torah as interpreted by Jesus can be fulfilled (Matthew). It is not a burden but the perfect law of liberty (James 1:25). Where missionary Gentile Christianity is dominant, we find a pessimistic anthropology: the Torah cannot be fulfilled (Paul).

5. Religions of Reconciliation and Religions of Redemption. A further typology distinguishes religions of reconciliation and religions of redemption. Buddhism is a typical religion of redemption; besides tribal religions, Judaism is a typical religion of reconciliation. Religions of redemption seek salvation through separation from the world, while religions of reconciliation seek it through cooperation within this world.

In religions of reconciliation, the world is the central stage of human conduct. This conduct involves neighbors, with whom one would like to get along well and with whom one must get along. Success and happiness are achieved in common or not at all. Insofar as conduct is good and supportive of the group, it is inherently meaningful. No additional transcendent meaning is necessary to reinforce it. Blessing is a consequence of conduct according to social norms, not actually a reward bestowed by invisible powers. Religions of redemption are different. Here the world is not the aim of conduct. On the contrary, it is necessary to be delivered from the world. Ethics is a-cosmic. The aim of good conduct is deliverance from the world. The individual does not act out of concern for the community and its well-being but to enjoy a better fate in the future. Neighbors are not valued for their own sake, for that would impose restrictive ties. Compassion, one of the highest virtues of Buddhism, is love without emotion and without connective engagement.

It does not take detailed analysis to show that Judaism is a classic religion of reconciliation. In apocalypticism, which longs for a new world, it incorporates elements of a religion of redemption, but these are still communal: apocalyptic hope does not look for the salvation of the individual but for a new world for the community.

Early Christianity occupies an intermediate position. In Jesus we still find features of a religion of reconciliation, even when they glow with apocalyptic longing for the kingdom of God. In the Gospel of John, however, Christianity takes the form of a religion of redemption, albeit still dominated by the idea of love, which creates a community here and now. Characteristic of early Christianity is its intermediate position between the prophetic religions of the West and the mystical religions of the East. By origin it belongs entirely within the traditions of a religion of reconciliation. The crucial criterion, focus on the community of neighbors, is still present. But it takes on features of a religion of redemption—for instance, in the *Gospel of Thomas*, in which the community is greatly reduced in importance. This gospel shows that early Christianity was open to experiences acquired in quite different contexts.

Such typologies do show, however, that the fundamental motifs and convictions of Eastern and Western religions are very different. Do we not find in the religions of the West an affirmation of this world, in the religions of the East a denial of this world? But the Eastern religions also know a monistic affirmation of the world. If all things are pervaded by the absolute spirit (Brahman), all things are affirmed. And, furthermore, the world is radically overcome. The *Gospel of Thomas* also contains such polarities. We sometimes find a blunt denial of the world: "Whoever has come to understand the world has found only a corpse, and whoever has found a corpse is superior to the world" (*Gos. Thom.* 56). It would be hard to outdo this denial. At the same time, there is an almost pantheistic sense that all things are pervaded by the Deity: "Jesus said, It is I who am the light that is above them all. It is I who am the all. From me did the all come forth, and unto me did the all extend. Split a piece of wood, and I am there. Lift up a stone, and you will find me there" (*Gos. Thom.* 77). We find side by side both a longing to leave the world and an assurance of finding the Redeemer everywhere within the world. The a-cosmic contempt for the world recalls Buddhism; the pantheistic deification of the world recalls Hindu monism. Both have analogies within Christianity.

Let me emphasize once more: all typologies of religion are schematic. But it cannot be by accident that within the typologies of the scriptural religions Christianity occupies an intermediate position. Its association with the first part of the Bible, the Old Testament, clearly makes it a prophetic and theocentric religion. But in the second part of the Bible, the New Testament, it has from the start elements of a mystical and anthropocentric religion. It occupies an intermediate position between religions of reconciliation and religions of redemption. This intermediacy must not be thought of as a mark of privilege. On the contrary, it imposes a special obligation to build bridges of understanding between religions and to promote interfaith dialogue. To this task it brings a culture of theological reflection and a wealth of experience in dealing with its own internal pluralism in the ecumenical movement. It is present as a minority on every continent. It can be tolerant. But it is also burdened with traditions of intolerance.

In the following pages we first discuss how biblical traditions can contribute to the dialogue between Christianity and the two Western world religions, Judaism and Islam. Both are intimately connected with Christianity, both genetically and through mutual influence. Then we address the two Eastern world religions, Hinduism and Buddhism, which did not have close contact with Christianity until the modern period. Of course, there are many other religions as well, but we use these four as examples.

Judaism and the Bible: The Old Testament

Christianity is an offspring of Judaism; Judaism is its mother religion. Many fundamental biblical motifs that we find incarnate in the Christ-event have been operative in the fate of the people of Israel. We have learned most of them in that context: Israel is God's son, God's vicarious representative, witness and martyr to the truth; Israel is the people of the exodus, of repentance and return. Those who do not belong to the people of Israel can participate in this history (and thus in the motifs that belong to it) through the Jew Jesus of Nazareth. We may therefore say that for Christians Jesus vicariously represents Israel. Through him they are linked to the history of Israel. One of the most important conclusions reached by two centuries of historical-critical study of Jesus is the fact that he belonged to two religions: during his lifetime, he was a Jew who never doubted his Jewish identity; his ministry was set entirely within the context of Judaism, even though he came into conflict with other Jewish groups. After his death, he became the foundation of Christianity. Therefore, it makes little sense to minimize the significance of Jesus in dialogue with Judaism, for it is through Jesus above all that Christianity is linked with Judaism—though he is not the only link.

Christianity is also linked with Judaism by the Hebrew Bible, what the Christian church calls the Old Testament. When Christianity relates to its foundations, it is relating at the same time to another religion. This gives Christianity an opportunity. In order to show the relevance of the Bible in interfaith dialogue, it is important for people to learn to read the Old Testament in the twofold history of its reception—not only as a preliminary to the New Testament but also as a book embodying authentic religious experiences that continued on as legitimately in Judaism as in Christianity. The traditional Christian denigration of the Old Testament needs to be revised. This appreciation of the Old Testament has long been the property of theology, but it is not yet common knowledge. We may formulate and discuss two principles:

1. The Old Testament has its own value apart from its use in the New Testament. In many respects it is even superior to the New Testament.
2. The reasons cited for denigrating the Old Testament apply similarly to the New Testament. Fairness demands that we judge both by the same criteria. Today both must be approached with a critical stance.

The independent value of the Old Testament has to do with God, the world, and humankind—and with the failure with respect to all three it reflects.[3]

1. The Old Testament Is a Witness to Monotheism. The Old Testament is our fundamental document of monotheism. Its monotheism converges with the monotheism that became prevalent among Greek philosophers at about the same time. But for an entire nation of real people (not just a few intellectuals) to enter into an all-embracing dialogue with the one and only God, and to hope that someday all people would enter into this dialogue—that is something singular. That is an enduring fundamental experience for humankind. There is nothing comparable in the New Testament. The Old Testament's understanding of God cannot be surpassed by anything the New Testament has to say about God. Of course, one can say that in the Old Testament this dialogue with God remained limited to one nation. The particularism of this tie to a specific nation must be transcended, and that happens in the New Testament. But the New Testament continues the particularism. Anyone who criticizes the tie between God and God's people in the Old Testament must also criticize the tie that binds the New Testament God to God's community, even though one comes to belong to a nation or people differently than to a community: by birth rather than free decision. But both are forms of particularism, in tension with the universality of the one and only God. The understanding of God in *both* Testaments points beyond their particularism. We are still on the road to a truly universal belief in God.

2. The Old Testament Contains a Comprehensive Approach to the World. The Old Testament is superior in three areas: creation, history, and society. Astonishment at creation, at the very existence of anything at all, is expressed far more powerfully in the Old Testament than in the New. Only the Old Testament develops a comprehensive view of history that assigns responsibility for history to humanity. The great story of the nations is reflected in a prehistoric, poetic narrative. It is shown that not just kings but all the people of a nation share responsibility within this history—and that this history includes a constant readiness to move on, to leave a familiar home and commit to an exodus, a hope for something new. It also becomes clear that a longing for justice and the management of power drives this history. The horizon of the New Testament is narrower. Here we do not have the literature of a nation and an entire people but the literature of small groups. Much that a vital faith must take into account is absent. Only the Old Testament enshrines a conception of social justice and power, beyond the horizon of the parochial New Testament. We can therefore say that the public language of faith, with which it formulates its responsibility for the world, is inconceivable without the Old Testament.

3. The Old Testament Contains an Impressive Anthropological Language. The Old Testament is superior in its language depicting human experience. There is nothing in the New Testament comparable to the imposing language of prayer in the Psalms. When we publish the Psalms with the New Testament, it is clearly not because they are a prerequisite for understanding the New Testament but because their intense expression of personal religious experience has never been bettered. Neither does the New Testament use the language of eroticism, such as we find in the sensuous language of the Song of Solomon. The same is true of the language of pessimism in Ecclesiastes and the cry of suffering in Job. Ecclesiastes was the first book of the Bible that I read intensively when I was young. The presence in the Bible of a book with "nihilistic" overtones made it accessible to me. It would be correct to say that we can appropriate texts of the Old Testament only through critical interpretation and selection. That also holds for the New Testament. But without the Old Testament, expression of personal Christian faith would be impoverished.

4. The Old Testament Transcends Failure. The Old Testament interprets the relationship with God, with the world, and with itself as a history of failure. But the New Testament is also the history of a failure: the kingdom of God did not come, the second coming of the Lord did not take place. Without the context of the Old Testament, it is impossible to deal appropriately with the experience of failure. When the greatest New Testament scholar of the twentieth century, Rudolf Bultmann, interpreted the Old Testament as a history of failure, he was more correct than many of today's interpreters. I read his theory against a different background. I was greatly influenced by Karl Jaspers, for whom the word *failure* has a positive connotation. Only life's failures and the mind's doubts give us access to the absolute. If the Old Testament is the configured account of repeated failure ending in catastrophe, it expresses a truth about our lives in relation to God and humanity. It would be better to ask: Do we find in the New Testament a comparable power to describe, admit, and configure failure? The answer is yes: the cross stands at the middle of the New Testament. And the hope that it stands for is—historically speaking—a failed hope. The kingdom of God did not come. The second coming did not take place. With the help of the Old Testament, we can overcome such experiences of failure better than without it.

To understand the Old Testament, it is also important to realize that the New Testament incorporates it only selectively. The following thought experiment will make this clear: What would we know of the prophets if we had only the New Testament? We would think of them almost exclusively as heralds of messianic hopes. We would know that Elijah and Elisha performed miracles (Luke 4:25ff.). Of their social criticism and their battle for justice we would know nothing. The Old Testament incorporated into the New Testament is a one-sided extract from the Jewish Bible, reinterpreted in the light of early Christian beliefs. And yet the way the first Christians read and interpreted the Old Testament is still instructive today. They read it with critical eyes. They revered it as Scripture but did not keep all its commandments (such as mandatory circumcision and the dietary laws). Here we have a model that combines esteem for a religious tradition with willingness to treat it freely—a model for dealing with all theological and religious traditions, including the New Testament. If we were to disparage the fundamental theological value of the Old Testament on account of a few texts open to criticism, we would lose a model for how to be loyal to a religious tradition while criticizing it.

Quite apart from this free treatment of their own Bible, the first Christians were tied much more closely to the Old Testament than they stated explicitly. They shared with it the axiom of monotheism and all its fundamental motifs, for they lived within a tradition of continuity with the Old Testament documents, which shaped them profoundly. They shared with Jews the structures of an interpretation of history, the world, and humanity; they believed in creation, the hidden wisdom of God within it, its openness to miracles, the possibility of repentance and return, and much more. Their only difference with Judaism was that they saw all these motifs embodied in the figure of Jesus. Their second core conviction, belief in the Redeemer, separated them from Judaism. And this belief in redemption had enormous consequences, especially when it was opened to Gentiles.

When Jews converted to Christianity, they remained within their traditions. They could do so because they believed that they had finally found true Judaism. Gentiles, however, had to leave their religion behind. Their pre-Christian lives therefore necessarily appeared "darker," lost in error. And their conversion demanded a more radical transformation of their lives. Therefore, we find in early Christianity, on the one hand, a deep pessimism as to the natural state of humanity. And on the other hand, we find a much greater "optimism" as to redemption, namely faith that individuals, through the Holy Spirit, could be inwardly transformed. The two go together: anthropological pessimism and radical assurance of redemption.

Jews thought differently in both regards. Instead of anthropological pessimism, they enjoyed a more "optimistic" biblical view of humanity, believing that God created humankind to fulfill the Torah. People are capable of fulfilling God's commandments. Jewish Christians shared this view of humanity. We find it in Matthew and the Epistle of James. According to Matthew, it is possible to carry out the law, especially if it is interpreted as humanely as Jesus did (Matt. 5:17ff.; 11:28ff.). Paul, however, believed human beings in their natural state incapable of fulfilling the law (Rom. 7:7ff.). They must be redeemed and transformed from *sarkic* ("fleshly," natural) beings to *pneumatic* ("spiritual") beings. Jews had to reject this optimistic belief in redemption on other grounds: Christians saw the beginning of redemption in inward transformation here and now, but Jews asked what had become of the redemption of the world. The world was still unredeemed. The Messiah had not yet come. On this point, Jews could express a profound pessimism, as in 2 Esdras at the end of the first century. Judaism remained a religion of reconciliation; Christianity developed into a religion of redemption.

But this cannot represent the defining difference between Jews and Christians. Early Christianity had within itself the heritage of a "religion of reconciliation." And in Judaism we find tendencies toward a religion of redemption. The separation between the two religions did not become lasting until Jesus was exalted to the status of a deity alongside the one and only God. The first Christians thus resolved the logical contradiction of monotheism: How can the omnipotence of the one and only God be reconciled with human suffering and human freedom? They identified within the Deity a suffering Son of God. God personally assumed the burden of human suffering, thus guaranteeing that suffering can be overcome. And they also ascribed divine status to the Spirit that fills human beings and makes them free. Even if the doctrine of the Trinity appears in the New Testament only in brief formulaic expressions (for instance, the command to baptize in Matt. 28:19), it is a natural outgrowth of the New Testament. Jews held fast instead to their consistent monotheism.

Traditionally, the defining difference between Judaism and Christianity has been seen in the description of Judaism as a religion of law and Christianity as a religion of grace. The New Testament scholar Joachim Jeremias, who was very sympathetic to Judaism, found this difference in the parable of the laborers in the vineyard when compared to rabbinic parallels: "In the parable of Jesus, the laborers who were engaged last show nothing to warrant a claim to a full day's wages; that they receive it is entirely due to the goodness of their employer. Thus in this apparently trivial detail lies the difference between two worlds: the world of merit, and the world of grace; the law contrasted with the gospel."[4] But a look at comparable rabbinic texts leads to a different conclusion. If we take the metaphor of reward as a starting point, we arrive at two fundamentally different interpretations: a reward can be appropriate remuneration ("fair pay") or an unearned gratuity ("honorarium"). An example of the first interpretation is *Sifra Behukkotai* (on Leviticus 26:9). In this parable, Israel's privileged status among the nations is justified on the grounds of its special commitment to God:

> "I will look with favor upon you" (Lev 26:9). They told a parable. Whom is this like? Like a king who hired many laborers. There was a laborer who labored many days for the king. The laborers came to receive their reward, and this laborer was among them. The king said to this laborer, "My son, I will look with favor upon you. The many who have done scant labor for me I will give scant reward. But to you I will reckon a great reward in the future." Thus Israel would ask its reward from God in this world, and the nations of the world [also] asked their reward from God. And God said to Israel, "My children, I will look with favor upon you. The nations of the world have done scant labor for me, and I will give them scant reward. But to you I will reckon a great reward in the future." Therefore it is written, "I will look with favor upon you" (Lev 26:9).

But another parable minimizes the principle of reward as a primary motivation for action (*Deuteronomy Rabbah* [*Ki Tetse*] 6:2 on Deuteronomy 22:6):

> Likewise: "Do not ponder the path of life" (Prov 5:6). R. Abba bar Kahana said: "The Holy One, blessed be He, says, 'Do not sit and ponder the commandments of the Torah. . . .' Do not say, 'Because this commandment is great, I will do it, for great is its reward; because this commandment is slight, I will not do it.'" What did the Holy One, blessed be He, do? He did not make known to His creatures the reward of each individual commandment, so that they would do each commandment in ignorance [of its reward], as it is written: 'Her paths wander, and she does not know it'

(Prov 5:6). Whom is this like? Like a king who hired laborers. And he took them immediately into his orchard and did not make known to them the rewards of the orchard, so that they would not neglect the work with scant reward and do [only] the work with great reward. In the evening he summoned one and said to him, 'Under which tree did you labor? That is a pepper tree; its reward is one gold piece.' And he summoned another [and] said to him, 'Under which tree did you labor?' And he said to him, 'Under this one.' He said to him, 'Its reward is half a gold piece; it is a caper tree.' He summoned another [and] said to him, 'Under which tree did you labor?' He said to him, 'Under this one.' He said to him, 'That is an olive tree; its reward is two hundred minas.' They said to him, 'Should it not have been needful to inform us which is the tree with the great reward, so that we could have labored under it?' The king said to them, 'If I had informed you which it is, would the whole orchard have been cultivated?'"

Comparable rabbinic texts even speak of God's grace to sinners. Here the vision of God's grace is even more radical than in Matthew 20:1-16 (*Midrash Psalms* 3.3.19a on Daniel 9:9):

According to the custom of the world, [if] a laborer labors with integrity for the owner and he gives him his reward, what thanks does he have? And when is thanks due? In the hour when he has not labored with integrity for him and he [nevertheless] does not withhold his reward. Therefore it is written, "To the Lord our God belong mercy and forgiveness, though we have rebelled against him" (Dan 9:9). R. Shmuel bar Nahmani said, "Have you ever seen that those who rebel against a king are [nevertheless] provided with food?" R. Jonathan said, "It is written, 'They made a calf at Horeb' (Ps 106:19). And [nevertheless] manna came down."

The parable of Jesus fits quite naturally within the spectrum of rabbinic parables. One of them even surpasses it in its radical vision of grace. Nevertheless, it has its own individuality. Not only does it have a more complex narrative structure—with distinct scenes, different groups of laborers, and a manager who mediates between the owner of the vineyard and the laborers—it also makes more complex use of the reward metaphor. Justice (Matt. 20:4) is placed in direct contrast with God's generosity (20:14b-15).

Thus, the two aspects of the metaphor, which appear separately in the rabbinic material, are brought together. The parable of Jesus shifts the appeal to the interpersonal plane:

> whereas in the rabbinic parables all Israel is always on the side either of the workers who labor honestly (in contrast to the Gentiles) or the workers who fail, Jesus differentiates within his Jewish audience. Those who do their utmost to fulfill God's will (for instance, the Pharisees) receive their reward, but at the same time they are asked to react "with a gracious eye" to God's goodness towards the less perfect (for instance, the toll collectors and prostitutes) and not be like the grumbling workers.

So much is clear: it is not emphasis on law or grace that separates Judaism and Christianity; both are familiar with God's grace. This point can be illustrated quite clearly in the differing actualizations of the same narrative material in Jesus' parables and rabbinic parables.

Islam and the Bible: God and Jesus in the Qur'an

While Christianity shares with Judaism the bulk of its Scriptures and is itself an offspring of Judaism, both Christianity and Judaism were forces behind the emergence of Islam. Looking back at Moses, the prophets, and Jesus, Islam could view itself as their consummation. Muhammad viewed himself as the last prophet: the Paraclete prophesied by Jesus, who would lead into all truth (John 16:13), and the "seal of the prophets," after whom there could come no other prophet. Muhammad adopted many biblical traditions. The corresponding passages in the Qur'an are a fruitful field for Bible teaching. Christians can learn much from them about the fundamental problems of their monotheistic faith, and about their understanding of Jesus and of humanity.

The Islamic Understanding of God. Muhammad espoused a consistent monotheism that closely resembles Jewish monotheism—except that the latter remained linked to a particular nation, whereas Islam opened itself to all nations. This universalization it shares with Christianity, but it rejected Christian belief in the Trinity, through which—Islam believes—Christians commit the sin of *shirk* ("partnership"). Surah 112 of the Qur'an, the fundamental confession of faith used by Muslims, illustrates the anti-Trinitarian animus of the Islamic understanding of God: "Say: He is the one God, the eternal God. He begets not, nor was He begotten, and none is comparable to Him." It is understandable that belief in the universal God on the part of Muslims is viewed as the high point in the development of a pure belief in God. Islam succeeded in making viable the problem of theodicy exacerbated by monotheism without espousing any of the three positions that theology has repeatedly been tempted to take: undue assignment of responsibility for evil to God, humankind, or demonic beings.

1. Islam's anthropology is not pessimistic. It does not exaggerate human awareness of sin in order to account for evil, as though all the evil in the world derived from human sin. Propitiatory sacrifice and the propitiatory death of Jesus are therefore superfluous. As God created human beings, they are open to divine "guidance." They are not hopelessly corrupt, even though Islam is extremely sensible of human weakness and sinfulness. Human beings are inconstant and weak, but only Iblis (Satan) is bereft of hope. Islam rejects the notion of vicarious substitution; see Surah 39:7: "No burdened [soul] shall bear the burden of another."
2. Demons do not constitute an independent reality. Islam does not explain evil by making a demonized world responsible for it. The *diabolos* has become Iblis in the Qur'an, but he is a fallen angel, who rebelled against God. He does not possess any independent power alongside God.
3. Contrary to Christian prejudices, the Muslim understanding of God is not demonized. Texts in the Qur'an that speak of arbitrary predestination of individuals to salvation or damnation turn out on closer examination to speak of God's response to human conduct. Allah is the almighty and merciful, not a despotic tyrant.

How did this monotheistic conception become possible? Here we come face to face with two features of Islamic belief. On the one hand there is *Islam* itself, submission to the incomprehensible and sovereign God, to whom humans owe infinite trust despite all life's hardships. In the Islamic world, the power of such a simple faith is lived by multitudes every day; it deserves the recognition of other religions. On the other hand there is the *Islamic ethos*, which is more robust than either the Jewish or the Christian ethos. God is measured by this more "realistic" ethos. The aversion of the biblical God to the use of force, a conflict that pervades the entire Bible, was not incorporated into the Islamic understanding of God. The traditions of the holy war that we find in the Old Testament were revived. The difference between the Judeo-Christian understanding of martyrdom and the Islamic understanding is characteristic: in Judaism and Christianity, martyrs choose death rather than renounce their faith. They suffer violence but never commit violence. In Islam, however, martyrs are those who fall in the war against unbelievers. Rejection of the use of force plays a much smaller role in the shaping of Islam's understanding of God and humanity; this undoubtedly makes the Islamic ethos closer to the facts of real life than the Judeo-Christian ethos, with which it otherwise has much in common. These more "robust" ethical criteria reduce the tension between God's mercy and God's omnipotence; what tension remains is overcome by trust in God and submission to God. The Islamic understanding of God is much more able to reconcile mercy with severity than that of Christianity. For this very reason, the ethos of Islam deserves our understanding. It lacks the excessive demands for altruism found in Christianity, which leave a deep sense of guilt because of their impossibility. And this difference explains in turn some features of the Islamic understanding of Jesus.

Islam Rightly Views Jesus as a Prophet with a Theocentric Message.
Muhammad espoused a view of Jesus shaped by his own religious experience. Jesus and his disciples were for him exemplary Muslims. Jesus preached as a prophet sent by God. He healed the blind, cured lepers, and restored the dead to new life (5:110). His message was theocentric: "When Jesus came with clear signs, he said, 'I have come to you with wisdom and to make clear to you some of the points on which you differ. Therefore fear Allah and obey me. For Allah, He is my Lord and your Lord. So serve him; this is a right path'" (46:63-64).

Jesus himself was an exemplary embodiment of the virtues of a Muslim: prayer, almsgiving, and devotion to his mother. He says to Mary: "Surely I am a servant of Allah. He has given me the book and made me a prophet. And He has made me blessed wherever I may be, and has enjoined on me prayer and almsgiving as long as I live. And love for my mother; and He has not made me overbearing or wretched. Peace on me on the day I was born and on the day I die and on the day when I am raised to life" (19:30-33). Jesus identifies himself in the series of revelations before and after him: "O ye children of Israel, lo, I am the messenger of Allah to you, confirming the Torah that was before me and proclaiming the good news of a messenger who will come after me, whose name is Ahmad" (61:6).

But Islam also preserves the message of an individual whose birth and death were miraculous. Muhammad invoked not only Jesus' teaching but also his life and showed particular interest in the beginning and end of that life. Muhammad recognized both the virgin birth and Jesus' exaltation to the presence of God after his earthly ministry.

Jesus was the son of Mary. He was created by God in Mary's womb. His birth of a virgin does not mean that he was begotten by God. Quite the contrary: God created Jesus through God's spirit and word. Therefore, Christ can be called the word, or *logos*, without being set alongside God, as in the prologue to John. The fourth surah, in which Jesus is called the word, expressly cautions Christians against such a divinization of Jesus: "O people of the Scripture, commit no excesses in your religion, and speak only the truth concerning Allah. The Messiah Jesus, the son of Mary, was only a messenger of Allah, and His word, which he conveyed to Mary, and a spirit from Him. So believe in Allah and His messengers, and do not say, 'Three'" (4:171). The creative power of God is also alive in Jesus. From apocryphal stories of Jesus' childhood (*Gos. Thom.* 2:2-4), Muhammad borrowed the legend that tells how Jesus formed birds from clay and breathed life into them (3:49; 5:110). For it is fundamentally true: "It is not befitting Allah to beget a son, glory be to Him! When He determines a matter, He only says to it, 'Be,' and it is" (19:35).

Jesus met opposition and was accused of magic (5:110; 61:6). The Jews sought to kill him but crucified another in his place: "But they did not kill him, nor did they crucify him, but someone like him . . . [and therefore we cursed them]. And lo, those who disagree concerning him are truly in doubt concerning him. They know nothing of him but pursue only conjectures, for in reality they did not kill him. But rather Allah took him up to Himself, and Allah is mighty and wise" (4:157-58). Here Muhammad is probably borrowing a Gnostic tradition that Simon of Cyrene was confused with Jesus and was crucified instead of him, though it is also conceivable that Muhammad had come into contact with later theories concerning Jesus' death that taught that, although Christ did die, his body did not suffer or decay. This may have suggested erroneously to Muhammad that Jesus did not die. Either way, Muhammad's intent is to keep Jesus above all suffering, humiliation, and weakness. Elsewhere, however, he refers to Jesus' death—probably a natural death. He saw no salvific significance in Jesus' death. Such an interpretation would have run counter to his anthropology and his idea of salvation. Through his guidance, Allah gives the individual the opportunity for salvation. It is not necessary that someone die for the sins of the world in order to achieve salvation. Muhammad rejected the idea of Jesus' atoning death, in all probability a post-Easter christological conception. Only after Easter did the disciples overcome the shattering event of the cross by seeing in Jesus not just the last prophet (and first embodiment) of the kingdom of God but also the Redeemer who died for the sins of all.

Only after Easter did Paul develop a pessimistic anthropology based on his own experience, which led to a deeper understanding of the cross, an anthropology that let redemption shine all the brighter. This is the point at which Islam and Christianity diverge. Christianity (for the most part) thinks more pessimistically of the chasm between God and humanity, needing to be redeemed by victory over sin. In a word, Christianity must set a single individual in proximity to God in order to overcome the distance separating all humanity from God. In the eyes of Muslims, it thus commits the sin of "partnership," departing from strict monotheism. Although the tension between God's nearness and distance shapes both religions, Christianity differs from Islam in seeing a greater distance of sinful humanity from God and a greater nearness of God to redeemed humanity.

When Muhammad describes Jesus as a prophet and a messenger of God and calls Jesus' disciples Muslims (3:52; 5:111), when he has him taught from the Book (3:48), when he ascribes to Jesus the admonition not to forsake belief in the one God and turn to belief in three deities (4:171)—then the message of Jesus is Muhammad's own message. As the last prophet, Muhammad renews Jesus' message after it had fallen into oblivion among Christians. Ignoring Jesus' own warnings, they had constructed a "high Christology" that placed Jesus alongside God. In early Christianity there were groups of Jewish Christians who did not go along with a "high Christology." For them Jesus was simply a human individual. Did such Jewish-Christian traditions survive to the time of Muhammad? But Muhammad did affirm the virgin birth. Many Jewish Christians rejected it. For them Jesus was born of Joseph and Mary. Origen, however, knew of Jewish Christians who recognized the virgin birth (*Contra Celsus* 5.611) as well as those who rejected it (*Homiliae in Lucam* 17). It is therefore possible that Muhammad read Jewish Christian traditions about Jesus in the light of his own experience and that his views were reinforced by these traditions. This explanation is not certain. As he developed his understanding of Jesus, he could also have understood Jesus' message correctly without reference to existing traditions: it was theocentric. Jesus proclaimed the kingdom of God, not his own kingdom. His message of the kingdom of God is radical monotheism. The promise implicit in belief in the one and only God—that God alone will rule—finally will come to pass.

Islam Can Find a Relative Truth in the Biblical Religions. Although in the eyes of Muslims Christians commit the sin of "partnership," Islam can tolerate Jews and Christians. The limit of this tolerance is that Christians and Jews may convert to Islam, but a Muslim may not convert to Christianity or Judaism. Adherents of the scriptural religions may live in Islamic states but only as second-class citizens. This limited Islamic tolerance can be illustrated by a biblical text from Matthew 20:1-16 that also appears in Islamic tradition, where it refers to the relationship of the three scriptural religions:

> The messenger of God speaks: You and the owner of the two books before you [Jews and Christians] are like a man who hired laborers. He said, "Who will work for me from sunrise to midday for a qirat?" So the Jews worked. Then he said, "Who will work for me from midday to the time of afternoon prayers for a qirat?" So the Christians worked. Then he said, "Who will work for me from afternoon to sunset for two qirats?" So you work. Now the Jews and Christians became angry and said, "We have done more work and received less pay." God said, "Have I cheated you?" "No," they replied. Then God said, "This is my bounty..., which I give to whomever I will."[5]

When we compare this text with Matthew 20:1-16, we note that in the Islamic version the laborers do not receive the same pay; the last receive a double reward even though they worked for a shorter time. Despite this sense of Islamic privilege, the merits of the other religions are fully acknowledged. God gives Jews and Christians what they have earned. Muslims merely complete what the others began. The parable vividly expresses Islam's sense of being a culmination. It is balanced by a sense of commonality: Jews, Christians, and Muslims labor in the same vineyard of the Lord. They do the same work. The special privilege accorded Muslims is pure grace. Their additional reward is a free bounty to which they have no claim. Jews and Christians are placed in an unfavorable light not because their work (their religion) is worthless but because they are angry at the Muslims. They cannot simply acknowledge that God has freely shown his special grace and favor to the Muslims as the last to work in his vineyard. Jesus also criticizes the complaints of the others, but in his parable it is the equal treatment of all that creates ill will.

Jesus was not thinking of different religions. But early Christianity could already have applied the parable to Jews, Jewish Christians, and Gentile Christians. At least this is one common traditional interpretation of Matthew 20:1-16: even the Evangelist may have interpreted it in this sense. With the aid of Christian traditions (read in the light of their reception by Islam), we could go a step further: Must not all religions acknowledge that God has the freedom to treat them alike? Must not everyone learn to acknowledge that others are different without becoming emotionally upset? Must not everyone recognize the "good work" done by others and be content with the same "reward"?

The Bible links Judaism and Islam with Christianity. Anyone interested in dialogue with these religions has a motive to study it and will read it with new eyes in the light of its Jewish and Islamic interpretation. But what about the mystical religions of the East? They have come to know the Bible only in recent times. As mystical religions, furthermore, they are structurally quite different from the religions of the West. Can there be a fruitful encounter with them? We have already seen that there is an underground stream of mysticism in all the biblical religions. It was present in Christianity almost from the outset. As early as the second century, Christianity faced a mystical reinterpretation, that of Gnosticism. Does this strain of mysticism give Christianity a closer tie to the Eastern religions than the other biblical religions have?

Hinduism and the Bible: Ahimsa and Nonviolence

Hinduism is a collective name for a wealth of religions native to the Indian subcontinent. A Hindu identity came about only through differentiation from foreign rulers: first Islamic, then British. The clash with Christian influences under British rule led to a renaissance of Hinduism. Ramakrishna (1834–1886) himself, one of the central figures of this renewal, had a vision of Christ. In 1893 his disciple Vivekananda addressed the World Parliament of Religions in Chicago with the message that all religions are true and India is the mother of religions. The Christian world was most impressed by Mahatma Gandhi (1869–1948), because he combined the ancient Indian tradition of *ahimsa* ("noninjury") with the nonviolence enjoined by the Sermon on the Mount, thus creating the concept of "nonviolent resistance."

The ancient Indian ethos of *ahimsa* arose from criticism of animal sacrifice and the notion of reincarnation: if living creatures embody souls of human beings reincarnate within them, they must not be injured. This ethos underwent further development in Jainism and Buddhism, the two monastic movements that emerged from Hinduism, but it lives on in Hinduism as well. Of course a deep respect for the sanctity of life is not the same as nonviolent resistance. Was this ethical concept an outgrowth of Gandhi's encounter with the Sermon on the Mount?

There is reason to be skeptical. The Sermon on the Mount expressly forbids resistance: "But I say to you, Do not resist an evildoer" (Matt. 5:39). Gandhi had to read past that. In other respects, too, his reading of the Sermon on the Mount was selective. He disregarded the prohibition of oaths. Self-commitment, oaths, and vows were for him important instruments in the struggle for liberation. Did he then use the Sermon on the Mount only superficially—perhaps only to remove a source of legitimation from the hands of his Christian adversaries in England and discomfit them? Or, while ignoring the tradition of Christian interpretation, did he discover something true when he read the fifth antithesis as a call to nonviolent resistance—not on the basis of historical-critical exegesis, but on the basis of his actual situation, which demanded protest and resistance? There is no space here to discuss all these problems in detail. I believe that Gandhi arrived intuitively at the correct reading. The nonviolence of the Sermon on the Mount hopes for change on the part of the adversary. But there is no consensus concerning this interpretation.

In the fifth antithesis of the Sermon on the Mount, Matthew gives four concrete examples of nonresistance. They concern immediate personal circumstances (not responding to a slap on the cheek), legal circumstances (distraint of a garment), exercise of political power (forced labor), and economic circumstances (charity and loans). The last admonition interrupts the train of thought: "Give to everyone who begs from you, and do not refuse anyone who wants to borrow from you" (Matt. 5:42). This is addressed to someone who has not suffered any wrong but is told instead to do good to others. A free gift may even create an obligation, and a loan can be called in. This example shows that the intent is not only to suffer the behavior of others but also to establish a future obligation.

The fifth antithesis is related thematically to the first, which has to do with overcoming one's own aggressions (inward anger). Both can be interpreted reciprocally. In the concrete examples Matthew uses to illustrate his first antithesis, an individual is made responsible for the behavior of others. If you realize as you approach the altar "that your brother or sister has something against you, leave your gift there before the altar and go; first be reconciled to your brother or sister, and then come and offer your gift" (Matt. 5:23-24). If Matthew 5:23-24 has to do with influencing the behavior of others, so, too, does the fifth antithesis. It would miss the point to object that the people in the fifth antithesis are powerless. This is simply not true in the case of lending money. And the final example in the first antithesis also presupposes just this situation: a person on the way to court who is afraid of being imprisoned for debt should be reconciled with the accuser while still on the way, thus influencing the accuser's behavior.

In the light of the final antithesis, renunciation of violence is a way of loving enemies and *imitatio Dei*. When God makes the sun rise on the evil and on the good, God is not endorsing the evil done by those who are evil; neither should those who imitate God endorse the unjust behavior of others.

The Sermon on the Mount urges a kind of "paradoxical intervention." In psychotherapy, such intervention consists in aggravating the symptom (the client's problem) in order to overcome it. For example, when the client complains how awful the world is, the therapist paints it in even darker colors, so that the client will finally reject the therapist's picture and emerge from his shell of lachrymose passivity. In the same vein, he should react to another's violent behavior by provoking even more, so as to interrupt the spiral of violence. Since Palestine harbored memories of successful passive nonviolent resistance to the Romans, it is quite possible that the third antithesis of the Sermon on the Mount is hoping for a change in the violent confrontation, without making conduct dependent on it. This is not yet the nonviolent political resistance of modern conflict strategy, but it is closer to it than passive endurance. Did Gandhi intuitively discover a truth? Did this make him closer to the historical message of the Sermon on the Mount than many Christian exegetes?

All this aside, we must take into account the different interpretive context in which Jesus is viewed from a Hindu perspective. Judaism and Islam see him in the setting of a linear view of history, which asks where revelation culminates: while Christians believe that Jesus represents this climax in the midst of history, when God for one moment gave a complete revelation of himself, Jews still await the culmination of history. Muslims believe that Jesus was a preliminary stage looking forward to the culmination of revelation in Muhammad. Gandhi, however, approaches Jesus quite differently: for him history is the cyclic return of timeless truth. He is not interested in whether or not there was a historic Jesus, any more than whether the Hindu god Rama actually lived. The traditions about them enshrine timeless truth, and that is what matters. Gandhi cannot comprehend the tie that links faith to history. His Hindu background made him very familiar with this independence of history. But there is some evidence that it was reinforced by the influence of theosophy—a modern religious movement that incorporated Buddhist theories about reincarnation—which he had encountered in London, and might have been as influential as the ancient traditions of India in shaping his politics of tolerance. In addition, his teaching can be seen as part of a universal international wisdom tradition.

This tradition also appears in the Bible. The Sermon on the Mount, with its rejection of violence and vengeance, echoes a wisdom tradition found among all peoples. The Sermon on the Mount makes it part of a goal-oriented view of history, for its demands are the condition for entry into the kingdom of God, imperatives marking a path through history to its goal. The inclusion of a timeless international imperative like the Golden Rule (Matt. 7:12) is therefore all the more remarkable. In Gandhi, then, many traditions converge: the Hindu tradition of nonviolence, esoteric theosophy, the Christian Sermon on the Mount, and a universal wisdom tradition that urges eschewal of vengeance and self-restraint as a way to deal with the hardships of life. Here, it would appear, we can find the universal in the specific. In a very elemental and fundamental ethics there are universal tendencies. The quest for them is of limited help in interfaith dialogue, but it would be wrong to minimize the value of such universal features. If there is ever to be a "world ethos," such traditions will be part of it. Encounter with Buddhism, however, brings us face to face with something that runs counter to all the principles of human behavior. And that is something we must take seriously.

Buddhism and the Bible: Anti-Darwinism as a Common Denominator?
Buddhism seems even more remote from early Christianity than Hinduism. At first only the differences are apparent. But both religions trace their origin to a founder. Both were shaped by historical figures. It is true that the earliest documents about the Buddha (who died between 420 and 350 B.C.E.) were not written until centuries after his death—even later than the inscriptions of the emperor Asoka (ca. 268–236/232 B.C.E.), the earliest witness of all, which date from more than a hundred years after the Buddha's death. But there is no doubt about his historicity. It was never a problem like the historicity of Jesus in Christianity. This is quite understandable, for it is religiously unimportant. All that matters is his teaching and the enlightenment it brings. This teaching is summarized in the four truths of suffering, its cause, its cure, and the path that leads to its cure. It is therefore reasonable to compare Jesus and Buddha by asking: What is their response to suffering? How do they see redemption from suffering?

Redemption from the Self and Its Transformation: The Response to Suffering. Anyone who reads the accounts of Jesus' healing miracles is apt to be disconcerted by their magical naïveté. But they express an elemental will to live that protests all misery and privation. They have strengthened this will through the ages: even the terminally ill are not abandoned. The disciples were commissioned to heal the sick. These miracle stories embody a protest against the principle of natural selection, which condemns to death (and extinction) life that is flawed in order that the fit may increase and multiply. The miracle stories disrupt this bitter competition to live. There is bread in such abundance that five thousand can eat their fill. The material necessities of life, which provoke conflicts and wars, are sufficient for all. The miracle motif—one of the fundamental convictions of the prophetic Western religions—proclaims an anti-Darwinian message.

In Buddhism we find a very different protest against the principle of natural selection, which is nevertheless related because it is a protest. This protest is illustrated by the story of the Buddha's excursions. The Buddha, a king's son, had been shielded from the sight of anything disturbing in the luxurious surroundings of his palace. On his first excursion in his chariot, he encounters an old man who had been left behind in the forest, "discarded like a worthless piece of wood." Quickly the Buddha has his chariot go back to the palace, where he diverts himself from the upsetting image with games and sex. On his second excursion, he meets a sick man "breathing with difficulty, with pallid extremities, failing organs, shriveled limbs, bloated body, suffering in agony, lying in his disgusting excrement." Again he returns to the palace, but he has lost his delight in games and sex. Finally, on his third excursion he meets a funeral procession. The mourners are weeping and wailing in their grief. They beat their breasts and scatter dust on their heads. Again the Buddha turns back—but this time to meditate on how to be set free from such evil. On his last excursion he meets a mendicant, and there ripens within himself a determination to give up the pleasures of the senses like the monk in order to live a life of self-control and seek "inward peace" in the life of a homeless beggar—free from passion and hatred. In his encounter with human suffering he had heard the call of the holy. He could not continue to live as before.

The Buddha's response to suffering is more philosophical and lofty than Jesus' response. Jesus seeks to heal the sick by using magical techniques and formulas designed to avert evil—although the miracle stories downplay them so as not to obscure the central point, which is resistance to hardship and suffering. The Buddha's response, by contrast, is characterized from start to finish by withdrawal, evasion. Initially he takes refuge in his royal palace, which will shield him from all forms of suffering. In the end he seeks a better refuge, the palace within, where suffering cannot penetrate. Always he seeks a place immune to all suffering. Jesus instead responds actively, almost aggressively. He wants to eliminate the suffering. And he himself is not immune to suffering: he dies in agony. The two attitudes are symptomatic of the outlooks dominant in two different cultures. But each attitude is also represented in the other culture. Western history is quite familiar with withdrawal from suffering into a monasticism dedicated to meditation and spirituality. And Buddhism is quite familiar with the compassion that besteads the unredeemed. But the dominant theme of the former is the will to eliminate suffering, and of the latter the search for a place within that is infinitely above suffering.

What the stories of Jesus and the Buddha express indirectly is also formulated discursively in the two traditions. According to Buddhist teaching, inner freedom from suffering comes only when one sees that the cause of suffering is a thirst for life. This thirst brings living creatures into conflict. Affirmation of being exposes us to suffering. Mere existence involves suffering, even if no catastrophe befalls, even if no guilt compromises life. To be is inherently to suffer. Therefore, liberation from suffering consists above all in seeing through the illusion of one's own self. The self is freed from suffering only when it "dissolves" and goes out like a candle.

This is the very opposite of self-redemption. It is more like redemption from the self, a gift of overwhelming enlightenment. Analogous New Testament texts about overcoming oneself speak instead of a higher form of the life for the self, not its dissolution. "If any want to become my followers, let them deny themselves and take up their cross and follow me. For those who want to save their life will lose it, and those who lose their life for my sake, and for the sake of the gospel, will save it" (Mark 8:34-36). True, this text also speaks of the desire for freedom from one's own self, but only in order to gain a higher form of life, not to be freed from the desire for life. The same is true of Paul, who writes: "For through the law I died to the law, so that I might *live* to God. I have been crucified with Christ; and it is no longer I who live, but it is Christ who *lives* in me" (Gal. 2:19-20). Here, too, the aim is to overcome the old self in order to have a higher form of life: Christ *lives* in me. The thirst for life is satisfied on a higher level, not conquered.

This difference must not be allowed to obscure the similarity. Buddhism has a worldview cognizant that all existence involves suffering. Everything causes some kind of pain. And the cause is the thirst for life that attaches itself to things. This is what makes us players in the great game of competition to live, in which we obstruct, supplant, and inflict suffering on each other. The Buddhist way of redemption seeks the path that leads out of this existence—suspension of the existence that competition and natural selection condemn to suffering. Christianity responds to the same desire, not by dropping out of the game of this world, but rather in the hope that the reality characterized by competition and natural selection can be reshaped so as to enable life that does not live at the expense of other life. In the struggle to reduce suffering, Christianity unleashes more initiatives than does Buddhism. It seeks to reshape the world. But the quiet way in which Buddhism overcomes suffering has an inner nobility that is even more evident when we examine the goal of this conquest of suffering.

Nirvana and the Reign of God: Redemption in Buddhism and Early Christianity. For Jesus and early Christianity, the conquest of suffering is an anticipation of a great cosmic transformation: the coming of the reign of God, which is a dramatization of monotheism. The reign of God is the state in which the one and only God finally holds full sway. God's dominion is favor shown to the sick and the weak, the lost and the outcast, the socially stigmatized and the stranger. An infinite will that affirms life will prevail against all obstacles and establish justice, so that those who have been cheated of their lives will finally be able to live. The one and only God of the Bible, that infinite center of ethical energy, will pervade the whole world and wipe away all tears. The expectation that God's reign would come soon was not fulfilled. It was shattered. It will always be vulnerable throughout the course of history.

Nothing, however, can confute the Buddhist expectation of salvation. Drifting away in Nirvana through the extinction of the self is effectively a positive reinterpretation of what we shrink from in our Western religions: vanishing into nothingness. And yet it is more than nothingness. Nirvana is imperishable and unchangeable; it is like an empty space. It is indestructible, both close to and far from everything. It is pure peace—uncaused, infinite, indestructible. Both nothing and at the same time a blissful something. Much time could be spent characterizing it in the manner of a *theologia negativa*—that is, describing what it is *not*. The crucial point is this: Nirvana is without content because any concrete content would mean suffering. Even the distinction between consciousness and what it is conscious of would mean division and limitation. Therefore, Nirvana is a happiness that cannot even be experienced—and that might be the very pinnacle of happiness.

Perhaps we could put the difference as follows: in the expectation of the kingdom of God, the infinite vital energy of the one and only God prevails against all the forces that are hostile to life, whether (as sin) they lie in the human heart or (as demons) they threaten the world. Nirvana, however, is complete liberation from vital energy as the cause of suffering. And yet the two ideas converge. Paul says that at the end God will be all in all (1 Cor. 15:28). If this image can be understood as a kind of eschatological pantheism, at the end God would be the one and only reality, pervading and embodying all things. There would be only God and nothing else. The joyful realism of our descriptions of paradise would be gone, but so would the horrific realism of our fantasies of hell. By this path we would come to the completely undifferentiated reality that, like Nirvana, frustrates all thought that would describe it concretely. Convergence of ideas is not identity, but it is a vehicle for understanding: the Buddhist idea of Nirvana converges with Christian hopes for salvation if they are ruled by the prohibition of images. The nature of our being in death cannot be represented by an image or metaphor, any more than we can make an image of God. What awaits Christians there is nothing other than God. Could it be that dialogue with Buddhism might help Christians face an understanding of the beyond free of anthropomorphic representations, which has long been the belief of many Christians?

Religions are historically mature constructs. They cannot be changed by arbitrary ideas. If they lose their identity, they lose their motivating power. Therefore, assemblages taken from diverse religions are usually what German writer H. D. Hüsch called just passing "religious fads or metaphysical gimmicks." But the deep affinity displayed by Buddhism and Christianity in their revolt against natural selection and their consistent refusal to affirm a bitter struggle for life may enable each to enrich the other. Or, to put it more cautiously: in its conformation of life as resistance to suffering, I find Christianity more persuasive; in its acceptance of death as the end of all suffering, I lean toward Buddhism. Nirvana is the dark silhouette of God, which can suddenly become light. Buddha and Jesus—their followers believe that both have pioneered this path.

In the case of Buddhism, too, we can study the reception of the Bible only in the present. I will limit myself to an example from personal experience. Toward the end of the 1970s, I came to know the Japanese psychotherapist Yuzo Watanabe. He had originally been a Buddhist. While he was dealing with mentally ill patients, he came upon the New Testament. In one of Jesus' parables, he found a defining and liberating truth. He became a Christian (in a very broad sense) and founded a "Community of the Friends of Jesus." To pursue the truth that he had found, he studied religion and New Testament exegesis. And what sort of truth was it? He recognized in himself and his patients an often-unconscious fear of self-evaluation, which drives people to use every means in their possession to assess themselves more positively than others. He found a solution to this fundamental problem in the parable of the laborers in the vineyard (Matt. 20:1-16), in which the owner rewards all the laborers equally regardless of how much work they have done. Through this parable he saw that people cannot define their own value by their accomplishments, by a preconceived standard, or by comparison with others.

This parable calls us to leave the path of self-evaluation based on accomplishment and welcome acceptance by Jesus as ultimate acceptance. Watanabe identified the task of overcoming the relativity of self-esteem and solving the problem of insecurity as a central task of all religion. And on the basis of his own experience, he knew only two consistent solutions to the problem: the Buddhist solution and the Christian solution. I may recognize that I am absolutely "worthless," that my individuality is an illusion and that the happiness I strive for is merely suffering and a thirst for life. Thus, Buddhism overcomes all doubt about self-esteem; I can trust that I have absolute value. In that case, too, I am freed from all doubt about self-esteem. This is what happens in the message of Jesus. What Watanabe found problematic was what Jesus said about the last judgment. For some time he preferred to use the methodology of historical criticism to label these sayings inauthentic. For us the important point is that, setting aside a fundamental difference, he had recognized something that Buddhism and Christianity have in common. Belief that the world is entirely an illusion (Buddhism) seems irreconcilable with belief in the created world as a very real place of probation. But both beliefs are approaches to an absolute certainty about oneself.

The Bible and a Pluralistic Theory of Religion

In discussing interfaith reading of the Bible, we have assumed that reading the Bible is worthwhile. But younger people may well ask us: Why should we study the Bible more diligently than the Talmud and Qur'an? Are there reasons to prefer the Bible? The case does not have to be argued within the church. There it provides an opportunity to engage in dialogue with God, so that Bible reading has "absolute value." But an open study of the Bible wants to involve outsiders as well. When we address them, do we have to be content with a general argument for Bible study based on cultural factors? The Bible is one of the foundations of our culture and has influenced so many people that it should be known and understood. There would certainly be many good reasons for reading this book—even if it is not considered the book above all others.

Nevertheless, the conflict among the scriptural religions over who possesses the truth is instructive for outsiders as well. If we look at the various approaches that seek to make plausible the superiority of Christianity and the Bible, we must conclude in all fairness that other religions have equally good reasons to present similar arguments for their own superiority. How one decides depends on one's religious faith. For outsiders, however, it is important to be able to follow and comprehend these various decisions, so as to understand the self-concept of the various religions. I have chosen three modes of argumentation to present in the pages that follow: Christianity as the culmination of a process of *development*, as a *synthesis* of diverse religions, or as an *anticipation* of the end. I shall then present my own position.

What religion is the culmination of religio-historical development? If we agree with German Idealism, as exemplified by Hegel, and understand history as the self-realization of God, who, following God's alienation in the world, becomes conscious of Godself once more in humanity, then Christianity is the culmination of this process of growing self-awareness on the part of the deity. For here we find (in the Gospel of John) the idea that deity and humanity are one (John 10:33). For those who think in such categories, Christianity (at least its Western core) is the absolute religion, the goal of the entire history of religions. It is surpassed only by philosophy, which conceptualizes what Christians believe as an idea.

To test this approach, let us examine Islam. If only because it is the latest of the great scriptural religions, it can make a plausible claim to being the culmination of previous religions. It could argue as follows: In Judaism belief in the one God remained limited to a single nation; in Christianity it was opened to all nations, but at the cost of accommodating paganism by deifying Jesus. In Judaism universalism was not yet fully developed, in Christianity monotheism was obscured. It remained for Islam to combine the strict monotheism of Judaism with the universalism of Christianity. Only in Islam is every remnant of paganism (in the form of associating other divine figures with God) vanquished. Muhammad is the "seal" of the prophets, the unsurpassable culmination of religio-historical development. Since Christianity is also in the process of retracting its "high Christology"—in part because of our knowledge of the historical Jesus, in part because of the independent emergence of devotion to the human figure of Jesus—we find here a convergent development leading to Islam.

A second approach asks whether a religion can be understood as a synthesis of other religions. Ernst Troeltsch argues as follows: All religions distinguish an ordinary world and a higher world. They can be assessed on the basis of how well they lead their followers to the higher world. Judaism and Islam, prophetic religions of the law, personalize human beings, confronting them with an absolute demand. Their limitation is that they require human beings to enter the higher world by their own efforts. In Hinduism and Buddhism, religions of redemption, the passage from one world to the other is made by inner enlightenment. Ultimately that is self-redemption. But their critical limitation is primarily that they do not have the personalizing effect of the prophetic religions. Only Christianity is both: a prophetic religion of redemption that combines the positive elements of both types of religion. Here believers are taken beyond themselves by pure grace!

Again let us test this claim. On the basis of its internal structure, Hinduism considers that it is best suited to being a synthesis of all religions. Behind the many deities of India it can see a single deity. It combines monotheistic and pantheistic, prophetic and mystical forms of religion. It needs only to apply its own synthetic power to all religions. In this spirit Vivekananda appeared before the World Parliament of Religions in

Chicago in 1893 with his claim that all religions are true and that India is the mother of all religions.

A third approach assesses religions according to how they anticipate the whole of history, so that they are able to incorporate their own historical nature in their self-conception. Wolfhart Pannenberg finds here a superiority on the part of Judaism and Christianity: both are aware of their own historical nature and both present a vision of history in its totality. For Christians, Jesus is the key to understanding all of history. History is like a text that has not been completed. We understand texts only when we have finished reading the whole text. In Christ, however, the end has already been anticipated as resurrection from the dead. He is the "prolepsis" in which there is already present what will one day be reality for all: resurrection and life.

This claim, too, we can test. Whoever believes that the end of history is not eternal life but absorption in Nirvana must give Buddhism credit for possessing the key to history—assuming that history cannot be understood apart from its end. One who meditates touches on Nirvana now and anticipates the end toward which all things move. Of course, the notion of history's end or goal is far removed from the cyclical thought of Buddhism. Nirvana is the end of the futile cycle of reincarnations, not the end of a linear history.

Let me here outline my own view. It cannot be more than a proposal. Religions, I believe, should be approached in two ways. First, they should be known and judged *ethically*, "by their fruits" (Matt. 7:16, 20); second, they must be respected *religiously* for their beliefs, even if these appear alien. An anti-Darwinian theory of culture gives us the ethical criterion by which we can measure them, and a hermeneutics of alienity gives us the ability to respect them where they differ from us. In addition, religions must not surrender their own core for the sake of all other religions; they have an obligation constantly to interpret it afresh, for themselves and for others. The need to interpret it for others is a boon both for themselves and for the others. But in the realm of ethics, religions must seek out what they have in common, since they must cooperate with all other religions.

First, the ethical assessment of all religions. All religions, I believe, contribute to the task of reducing the force of natural selection. Culture begins by making human life possible where it could not survive under natural circumstances: the weak receive a chance to life that is the result of ethically motivated behavior and is made possible by technology. Nietzsche already saw in compassion a countervailing force to natural selection ("Pity thwarts the whole law of evolution, which is the law of natural selection. It preserves whatever is ripe for destruction"). He condemned it and Christianity with it: in the kingdom of God, the poor, the sick, the starving, and children truly come into their own. The early Christian miracle stories protest against the natural distribution of the opportunity for life by giving those on the margins of life a new opportunity. The ethics of Jesus marks a break with the behavioral tendencies of evolution throughout history: in biological evolution, we find family solidarity (that is, help and support among people who are genetically related) coupled with aggression against those who are genetically different. Jesus reverses this principle: he requires his followers to break with their families and to love their enemies. Here he crosses a threshold between an old world and a new, the threshold between biological and cultural evolution.

Not that it was crossed for the first time in Palestine. This threshold pervades all of history. But in ancient Palestine there emerged in apocalypticism an awareness that history is marked by transitions: in Daniel 7, the bestial kingdoms are displaced by the kingdom of one like a human being. The first Christians saw this figure in Jesus, the Son of Man, and saw the transition from an eon dominated by beasts to a more human world. They saw this transition taking place in their own day—and it takes place in every person whose behavior has escaped the principle of natural selection of the previous phase of evolution. The notion of the last judgment that separates the sheep from the goats feels archaic and cruel, but it reflects the pressure of natural selection that holds all life in thrall. All things are pressed to adapt to overall reality. Human life cannot meet the demands of this pressure.

The proclamation of grace and the forgiveness of sins, on the contrary, abolishes the pressure of natural selection. It chimes with this evolutionary interpretation that Jesus' cross and resurrection became the central message of Christianity. For evolution takes place through the unequal distribution of the opportunity for life—ultimately through death, which makes room for new varieties of life. When death is overcome, the principle of natural selection is overcome. When a crucified failure becomes the wellspring of life, evolution proceeds where it would have come to an end within biological reality. If reducing the pressure of natural selection is the secret program of all civilization, then Jesus stands at its hidden center.

With Jesus as starting point, we discover resistance to the pressure of natural selection in other religions. This resistance is a vital element of Judaism. God chooses the tiny nation of Israel, threatened on all sides by major powers and destined to vanish. Islam proclaims the mercy of Allah. The redemption religions of the East use nonviolence (*ahimsa*) to limit the struggle for the opportunity to live. Buddhism is strongly anti-Darwinian. But the crucial point is that in all religions we find a contest to decide whether religious energy is to be mobilized to overcome or to intensify the struggle to live. An invisible boundary runs through them all between those who follow the call to enter a new world and those who remain in thrall to the old. In all of them, one truth is constant: many are called, but few are chosen (Matt. 22:14).

The assessment of all religions by an ethical criterion is a search for a common denominator. Their assessment by a religious criterion, on the contrary, is meant to encourage them to develop and preserve their distinguishing characteristics. Each has something unique to contribute that enables dialogue with transcendence. The distinguishing characteristic of Christianity is belief in the triune God. This understanding of God, I believe, arises necessarily from the contradictions of the biblical understanding of God. In the Old Testament, the one and only God is an all-determining reality. God brings everything to pass, both good and evil. All "Western religions" share this belief. But it gives rise to two problems: the problem of suffering in this world and the problem of human freedom.

Belief in the triune God arises from the effort to deal with these problems. Other monotheistic religions may reject the answers of Christianity. But Christians have an obligation to interpret their own beliefs vis-à-vis Judaism and Islam: only the total immanence of God in Christ can bring the transcendent God to us in the face of suffering. Only the Holy Spirit can bestow freedom in the face of the omnipotent God. The Holy Spirit represents a spark of mysticism within Christianity. To reject this spark would erode the side of Christianity that helps give Christians a living appreciation of mystical religiosity. When Christians associate this Spirit with Christ rather than viewing it as a potential already present within people, they are affirming the historical transformation of humanity. Union with God is not an escape from history but part of that history in which God has been at work since creation. In short, belief in the triune God is the distinguishing characteristic of Christianity. With the Western religions, it commits Christianity to belief in God the Creator; with the Eastern, it commits Christianity to belief in the Holy Spirit. But belief in Jesus Christ distinguishes it from both. If a breakthrough to transcendence took place in him, Christians are obligated to bear witness to him. They can do so and still be convinced that other breakthroughs to transcendence take place elsewhere. Anyone who believes that humanity must not retreat to where it was before the Christ-event is a Christian.

Could this be a formula for dialogue among religions? For relationships between human beings, all are subject to the same ethical criteria; for relationship to transcendence, all respect their distinguishing religious characteristics. Could religions live side by side in "reconciled diversity" in this manner? This formula would not end the controversy over truth, but the debate would obey certain rules—which of course would have to be redefined repeatedly.

Where does this leave us? Here images are better than abstract ideas. Let us imagine that at the end of the ages the "Heavenly Academy of Sciences" is charged to select from all books and traditions whatever will be deemed true for all eternity. If we believe that the Bible in its core belongs in this "eternal canon," we affirm it as Holy Scripture. There is no reason that this canon cannot include texts from other religions. We do not know which they might be. We should remain open to the possibility that we would find many texts from other religions in this canon, but also to the possibility that it might not include the whole Bible! One criterion used by these heavenly scholars—perhaps not the only one—would be the extent to which the texts are committed to an anti-Darwinian spirit.

We have been able to discuss only a few aspects of learning in an interfaith setting. They should make clear that the goal of such learning is to preserve one's own identity in dialogue. Interfaith dialogue bears fruit only when all the participants respect and maintain their own identity and that of the others. Christology, which initially appears to be a stumbling block in this dialogue, must not be denied. It is part of Christian identity. If we can use Christology to find paths to an appreciation of other religions, we have rooted our dialogue with other religions in the core of Christian identity and done more to further it than is achieved by "removing the rough edges" of the Christian faith.

But openness to dialogue is furthered by a sensibility for the fundamental structures of the various religions—their hidden grammar, which is often easier to grasp intuitively than to reconstruct. This sensibility helps us repeatedly to see the agreement in fundamental beliefs that lies behind manifest differences. Within the prophetic religions of the West, this appears easy. Here, besides the basic conviction regarding monotheism, we find the same fundamental motifs, no matter what different shape they may take: miracles, wisdom, renewal, faith, judgment—all these appear in Judaism and Islam as well as Christianity. In dialogue with the mystical religions of the East, these motifs are missing. We find analogs to them, but they are embedded in an interpretation of the world that surfaces in the prophetic religions only as a Gnostic and mystical countercurrent.

It is all the more important to recognize that diametrically opposite systems can embody the same fundamental anti-Darwinian approach. The symbols and images of all religions, I believe, fumble for the threshold that leads from biological evolution to cultural evolution. In the mystical redemption religions of the East, this process is interpreted as abolition of the world through redemption; in the prophetic reconciliation religions of the West, it is interpreted as consummation of the world through reconciliation. Within the framework of these overall interpretations, however, we find analogs to many fundamental motifs: repentance, atonement, and return appear in the East as enlightenment. Love and mercy appear as compassion, while wisdom appears as insight into the illusory nature of the world. Faith appears as dedication to one's spiritual master, reversal of status as the asocial monastic way of life, and so forth. If we go beyond the surface of religions and explore their hidden grammar, we can recognize in the alien aspects the otherness within ourselves without assimilating it. But is affirmation of otherness possible? Is it possible without forcing the traditional religions to give up their claims to absolute truth? There has been some experience of this possibility within Christendom: ecumenical dialogue. Here Catholicism constantly reasserts its absolute claims, but these claims are infiltrated by actual practice. We turn now to this dialogue.

THE BIBLE IN INTERCONFESSIONAL DIALOGUE

Christianity brings a valuable experience to interfaith dialogue: ecumenical dialogue, which has a tradition of dealing with almost insoluble contradictions and high tolerance for frustration in facing outdated claims of absolute truth. Within Christendom, too, it long appeared impossible for a history of misunderstanding, hatred, and war to give way to a history of dialogue and understanding. And the Bible has played an important role in this transformation. All denominations and confessions appeal to the Bible. They all share its premises and fundamental motifs. It is the basis for their sense of commonality, while it also legitimates their differences. In a confessionally pluralistic world, therefore, biblical study and teaching will interpret the Bible in such a way as to account for its differing interpretations in different churches and denominations. And conversely: the Bible must be taught with all its internal pluralism, which is even greater than the multiplicity of Christian churches and communities. Its multiplicity illustrates movements within Christianity that run athwart traditional ecclesiastical boundaries: liberation theology and fundamentalism, feminist theology, Jewish-Christian dialogue—all reflect the riches contained in Scripture.

Within the Bible, we find images of peaceful coexistence with neighbors in the patriarchal narratives and an ideology of military conquest in the account of the occupation of Canaan; we find a Temple-centered piety alongside a secular wisdom that eavesdrops on life. We find prophetic protest against the powerful and a court-centered ideology of self-glorifying power. We encounter the pessimism of Ecclesiastes and the eroticism of the Song of Songs. Many are so impressed by this plurality that they forgo any attempt to summarize the content of the Bible so as not to compromise its plenitude.

This plenitude has only expanded with the end of an interpretative approach that believed a text could have only one possible meaning. Today it is easier to accept a variety of readings. Hermeneutical civil war over the interpretation of a text is out of the question. If we could demonstrate convincingly to present-day readers why Protestants and Catholics, Lutherans and Orthodox, Baptists and Methodists, as well as Mormons, New Apostolics, and Jehovah's Witnesses, can relate to the same Scriptures in different ways, it would contribute to understanding in a pluralistic society. This holds true even if one cannot accept all interpretations and believes there are good reasons for rejecting some of them. In any case, Bible study serves the cause of mutual understanding today. It is impossible in the present context to lay out a full program for such interconfessional Bible study; here we shall merely outline the task.

In secular dialogue, the distinguishing characteristic of a religious interpretation of life is the dependence of all life on an ultimate reality: God. In interfaith dialogue, Christian identity is manifest in the place occupied by Jesus Christ. In interconfessional dialogue, however, the distinguishing Protestant characteristic is trust in the Spirit. Such trust justifies the typically Protestant depreciation of the church, ministerial office, and the letter, but itself becomes a problem in the history of Protestantism, because the revolt against the medieval Catholic Church appealed to Scripture. Led by the Spirit (and independent of any ecclesiastical authority), people claimed the ability to decide questions of belief for themselves. The beginning of Protestantism is marked by a critique of authority. This critique has shaped Protestantism to the present day, insofar as Protestant vitality is not extinct. This Protestant principle can be defined in more detail, both positively and negatively.

Positively, it is trust in the "Spirit of God," who transforms the human heart and creates within it evidence of what is important for life with God. This evidence cannot be produced by coercion. It cannot be imposed as a moral requirement. It cannot be demonstrated through arguments. It is a creature of God's Word, which operates free of all physical and mental coercion. The only possible response to it is existential trust: the faith that finds access to God through Christ. It is not the outward Word itself that creates assurance; assurance comes only when the outward Word is illuminated by an inward word, by the inward witness of the Holy Spirit. Everything about religion and the church is dust and ashes if it is not quickened by this Spirit. Anything that would quench the Spirit is a corruption of religion. It could well be said that Protestantism is a religion of the Spirit and of freedom.

The Protestant principle, as described by Paul Tillich, can also be defined negatively as criticism of all attempts to make finite entities absolute. If the evidential experience created by the word of God stands at the heart of religion, there are three fundamental errors: making human *authority* absolute, a tendency of traditional Catholicism; making the *letter* absolute, as Protestant fundamentalism does; and making one's own *works* absolute, as Protestant and Catholic moralism does. The Protestant principle is a criticism of such absolutes. It voices its criticism not only within the church but in society as a whole—as a refusal to let finite values stand as absolutes. But it addresses its criticism above all to Protestantism itself.

The Institution as Absolute: Catholicism and the Protestant Principle
The difference between Protestantism and Catholicism was trenchantly expressed by Friedrich Schleiermacher: "The difference between Protestantism and Catholicism [is that] the former makes the relationship of the individual to the church dependent on his relationship to Christ, whereas the latter makes the relationship of the individual to Christ dependent on his relationship to the church."[6] The same is true of the Bible: In Protestantism individuals define their relationship to the church on the basis of their understanding of the Bible. In Catholicism individuals define their relationship to the Bible on the basis of the teaching authority of the church.

Of course, we are speaking here of traditional Catholicism. Today there is a process within Catholicism that is moving it in a Protestant direction, with the result that within Catholicism, too, individuals decide for themselves what to believe and how to act. The Bible has received greater respect. Since Vatican II, biblical exegesis has been freed of its confessional chains. Historical criticism—a product of Protestantism—has entered into Catholic exegesis. Today it is hardly possible to tell whether a piece of biblical exegesis is Catholic or Protestant. Catholic and Protestant exegetes use the same methods and arguments and share the same errors. And criticism of institutional absolutism is often much more credible in modern Catholicism than in the Protestant tradition.

The Letter as Absolute: Fundamentalism and the Protestant Principle
Fundamentalism is a much greater threat to Protestantism, because it is rooted in the Protestant tradition. Protestantism began with a protest against the medieval church by appealing to the Bible. This use of the Bible to criticize authority was bound sooner or later to turn against the Bible

itself and its authority. The critical spirit cannot be confined. It produced historical criticism of the Bible. Never before in the history of the world did a religion examine its own foundations so critically while joining such criticism with deep loyalty to these very foundations. The intention was to make belief more honest and improve communication.

Because of this criticism, Protestantism is more than a "scriptural religion." It is a religion of the Spirit, not the letter. More important than the letter is the critical reading of Scripture—in classical Protestantism in the light of the Holy Spirit, in modern Protestantism in the light of historical criticism and reason. Therefore, we find in Protestantism a characteristic ambivalence toward the Bible. In classical Protestantism, on the one hand, the Bible has been used to criticize other authorities; in modern Protestantism, on the other hand, the Bible itself is criticized—both in confidence that the "spirit" of the Bible is communicated clearly and distinctly when the word is heard.

The way classical Protestantism approached the Bible necessarily made it an unassailable document, so as to legitimate Protestant objections to the late medieval church and defend them against the Counter-Reformation. The authority, sufficiency, and clarity of Scripture became a bulwark against Rome. Protestantism's own legitimacy was secured with the help of the doctrine of verbal inspiration. No wonder it is still alive today in fundamentalist movements within Protestantism. Here, however, this fundamentalism no longer serves as a protest against the Catholic Church but against the mentality of the modern world. We should recognize the relative merit of this fundamentalism: its power to resist an all-devouring modern civilization deserves respect. But it seeks this power by defending the letter. According to classical Protestantism, however, the *authority* of Scripture depends on the inward witness of the Holy Spirit—that is, on evidential experiences in which the spirit of the Bible seizes the reader or hearer. And despite all the convergences between secular humanism and the biblical faith, this is not always the spirit of the modern world. Fundamentalist criticism of the modern world should therefore be heard as a voice—especially when it is based not on a "doctrine of Scripture" but on a pious lifestyle. Again we employ the same criterion: Are the fundamental motifs of the Bible operative in this pious lifestyle and its concomitant understanding of Scripture, or have important motifs been left out?

"Works" as Absolute: Social Moralism and the Protestant Principle

Fundamentalism is a reaction to modern Protestant criticism of the Bible and the daring enterprise of exposing "Holy Scripture" to untrammeled scientific examination—trusting that again and again the spirit of the Bible will prevail, will speak to people and transform them. During the past century, biblical criticism has gone through two phases. The first phase was characterized by criticism of "ancient" ideas in the Bible. The debate over demythologization dominated discussion of the Bible among lay people and theologians in the 1950s and 1960s. Since about 1970, criticism has moved from criticizing ideas to criticizing values and norms—from "faith and understanding" to "faith and conduct," as Karl Barth noted. Whether or not we share a mythological worldview, whether we understand it literally or figuratively, does not challenge our moral identity. What does threaten our moral identity is to use the Bible to reinforce and continue traditions that have caused suffering and continue to cause suffering—for instance, when we pass along texts and traditions whose dark trail leads to Auschwitz. This shift to a morally committed reading of the Bible is always associated with the danger of "social moralism," a temptation facing all confessions and denominations.

Galatians 3:28, a familiar text, can serve as a starting point. Here Paul says that in Christ there is no longer Jew or Greek, slave or free, male or female. The words of this text stand in tension with the historical use of the Bible and other texts within the Bible. The result has been the emergence during the past thirty years of three dominant value-based readings of the Bible:

1. A reading that focuses on the relationship between Jews and Gentiles: exegesis in the setting of Christian-Jewish dialogue.
2. A reading that sides with the poor and underprivileged: as liberation theology, *minjung* theology, or a "theology of poverty."
3. A reading from the perspective of women: feminist exegesis.

Scholarly exegesis has often kept a respectable distance from the value-based interpretations. The proven ethos of historical criticism, which understands texts in their historical context rather than the context of the present, has been mobilized against a hermeneutics in the service of Israel, liberation theology, or feminism. This response is justified in many ways, but it has often been unwarranted. People frequently do not recognize that the problems we face today were already operative in the historical context of the past, even if under different conditions. Galatians 3:28 demonstrates the point.

Today we can see that this value-based hermeneutics has helped us discover much in the biblical texts that was formerly overlooked. Through it people who were previously underrepresented have taken part in dialogue about the Bible: Jews, the poor, women. If it is a long-held Protestant conviction that the fundamental statements and motifs of the Bible are accessible to all, that its spirit can authentically seize anyone, then Protestants must listen up when groups that have discovered their voice in the Bible (alongside the voice of their opponents) but cannot feel at home in the academic exegesis of the Bible press to be heard. Above all, it is in these committed readings of the Bible that Protestant criticism of making the letter an absolute is alive and well. In the face of texts that are anti-Jewish, politically oppressive, and patriarchal, they hold fast to a spirit of the Bible that moves beyond all borders and sets people free.

But these morally committed readings also illustrate the temptation of a moralism that makes specific values, imperatives, and acts the criterion of salvation. Protestantism came into being through criticism of salvation through works (in our relationship to God) but required works as an expression of love (in our relationship with others). Those who are freed from care concerning their own salvation should be free to address the cares of others and to act on their behalf. But this ethos can easily be corrupted: commitment to others becomes the mark of salvation—not its basis, but a sign that someone has found true life. This Protestant moralism is easy to recognize when it supports traditional behavior, less easy when it promotes modern values—justice, freedom, and equality. Besides the moralism of private decency there is also the moralism of progressive social morality, associated with a notoriously tender conscience, as though it were our duty to transform the world. When we are aware of this internal danger posed by moral engagement, we can safely say that Protestantism must maintain this social and moral unrest. It is a precious heritage. But when it is separated from confident assurance of salvation prior to any action or engagement, it can become self-destructive: making works an absolute, even the most just and necessary works, is to absolutize the finite. It is a target for criticism.

In the context of the Bible in ecumenical dialogue, we return once more to the parable of the laborers in the vineyard. The early church, as seen in Origen, interpreted the time of day theologically or morally. The various groups of laborers were the people of the age of Adam, Noah, Abraham, or Moses, while Christians constituted the last group. All were saved—but the next to last remain the last but one! Or the day represented the human life span. Many Christians have been Christians since childhood;; others become Christians on their deathbed. All have the opportunity to gain the one reward: eternal life. Since the Reformation, we can observe an exegesis of the parable in which Protestantism trumps Catholicism: the difference between law and gospel is projected into the parable. The grumblers who worked the whole day are people of the law, Catholics (or Jews), while those who receive full payment through the owner's generosity are people of faith (Protestants). The fact that all received the same reward is no longer the point, but rather that, according to Matthew 20:16 (probably a late secondary addition), the first (Catholics) will be last and the last (Protestants) will be first. Catholic exegesis, however, has always tried to read into the parable the Catholic doctrine of reward, which maintains that all are saved by grace, but according to their merit. Therefore, a gradation has to be found within the equal reward. This was the view of Thomas Aquinas: all share in the same bliss, but in varying degree. Or what the different groups of laborers had earned had to be represented as equal in value despite the different hours worked, so that the same reward for all stands to reason: those who came late are rewarded for their good intentions (as well as the work they did).

Impartial exegesis can show that neither interpretation fits the text. This parable does not represent God's justice and mercy as antithetical, as the Protestant reading tends to do. The owner of the vineyard acts justly and generously as well. Neither does the parable deal with merit versus grace, on which Protestants set such store, for the last received the same *reward* as the first!

The parable is most likely directed against human efforts to link God's justice and God's graciousness in such a way that one becomes the standard for the other. In that case either God *may* no longer be gracious, since the principle of justice forbids it, or God *must* be gracious to all, since the principle of equality dictates that all have an equal claim to graciousness. Thus, the parable is focused on a just God's *freedom* to be gracious. It does not offer a new system of unmerited graciousness that will take the place of the normal standards of a justice that grants to all what they have earned. Instead, the standard values are "disrupted" by the appearance of God's love, and they thereby lose their deadly universal validity. "I came not to call the righteous but sinners" (Mark 2:17). This description of Jesus' activity neither denies nor excludes the righteousness of the righteous. It simply brings God to those who need God, the sinners.

There is no basis in the parable for Protestant triumphalism vis-à-vis Catholics. It is closer to the gradualist school of thought in Catholicism, which sees God's mercy as surpassing his justice, than to the adversative thought of Protestantism, for which law and gospel are antithetical.

CONCLUSION

L et me sum up the preceding observations and arguments about why any educated person should come to know and appreciate the Bible. My central goal has been to convey the fundamental beliefs and motifs of the Bible. As we have seen, these alone are the ground of Christian identity. If they are not clear, dialogue in a multicultural world is impossible. But Christian identity must also be defined in such a way as to be capable of dialogue.

I also have been concerned with discussing the coherence of the Bible in such a way as to describe the contours of a "biblical identity," whether or not it springs from religious belief. My choice of relatively formal core themes is intended to serve this purpose. They make it possible to discover convergences and differences between biblical and secular humanism, or between different religions and different denominations, without denying that what is distinctive to biblical faith is reference to God, to Christ, and to the Holy Spirit.

Let me address once again the question of how the biblical materials shape and constrain Christian identity. Instead of treating the question abstractly, I will use a metaphor: the Bible is a great story, a tale whose end has not yet been written. It can be likened to the assignments teachers often give students when teaching language and literature: take the beginning of a story and continue it to the end. The teacher is testing whether students have intuitively grasped the norms of the genre and are able to use narrative motifs appropriately. Stories that do both are acceptable continuations. Some will be better, some worse, but there are no obligatory continuations. The situation is similar with regard to the great biblical story. The ways in which we continue it in our own lives shows whether, and to what extent, we have intuitively understood the narrative norms and motifs of the Bible correctly. We can raise them to the level of consciousness, by outlining biblical beliefs and motifs as I have done here. If enough of these are clearly operative in our lives, we may say that our continuation of the biblical story is appropriate to a "biblical identity." If we find these norms and motifs are not operative, we may say that our own stories reflect a loss or erosion of biblical identity—and that necessarily means an erosion of Christian identity as well.

In our continuation of the biblical story, naturally we are in a different situation than students finishing a story, for students have a teacher to evaluate and correct their efforts. The teacher knows the norms of the genre and the narrative motifs—as well as the end of the story. We, however, have to work out the dominant motifs and core convictions for ourselves in dialogue about the Bible. We do not know how the story ends. We are like the imaginary members of a "Heavenly Academy of Sciences," whose job it is, looking back over history, to sift all texts and traditions to find out what they contain that is of value. In our discussion of the biblical tradition, we anticipate the "domination-free communication" that historically has been impossible under "earthly" conditions but is operative as a regulative ideal.

In this understanding of Christian identity as a participation in a biblical identity, it is unimportant how much historical truth we ascribe to the narratives and texts of the Bible. What matters is whether we have the confidence to live in the third millennium with the fundamental motifs they contain; whether these motifs enable us to interpret the world persuasively; and whether, in the process, they make available something that is indispensable for human life.

The biblical texts leave no doubt about what that something is. From the Christian point of view, it may be summarized in three points.

1. Biblical texts promise that they can help us make contact with an ultimate reality. The Bible is an opportunity to enter into dialogue with God. To those who internalize its fundamental motifs and are transformed by them, the Bible promises that the reality of God is disclosed, as when a hidden figure suddenly appears in a confusing puzzle picture, once our eyes have been opened to it.

2. The Christian claim is, further, that all the motifs and fundamental beliefs (what we have called the "spirit of the Bible") appear not only in texts but also incarnate in a human figure: Jesus. In him the *Logos* became flesh. We may understand this mythological statement as follows: All the motifs through which God's reality is disclosed are

reflected in Christology. These motifs are the light that enlightens everyone (John 1:9). In Christ this light has been made accessible to all. He opens that path to the Father. He transforms those who trust in him, so that they experience reality differently than before their transformation.

3. The spirit of the Bible blows where it chooses. When it transforms human hearts, each person has an immediate relationship with God. Of course, this relationship must be examined in dialogue with others and reflected on with the help of the church's tradition. But for Protestants it needs no authoritative tutoring by an ecclesiastical magisterium—although dialogic instruction could be helpful. The "spirit of the Bible" is tied to the letter (though not identical with it), not to ecclesiastical authority. Through this spirit even Jesus was transformed—from a "master" to a "brother."

This is therefore the potential of biblical identity at the start of the third millennium: the possibility that biblical texts may communicate the fundamental motifs of thought, experience, and action that enable what Christian faith traditionally has called dialogue with God, a living relationship with Jesus, and a life transformed by the Spirit. Following the classical tradition of the church, we can label this crucial core with the terms *God*, *Christ*, and *Holy Spirit*.

But this potential can be realized only if all of us, Christians and non-Christians alike, approach the biblical story with a spirit of self-critical awareness and openness to genuine dialogue. On the part of Christians, such dialogue cannot be motivated by the aim of making others into adherents to the Christian faith, but by the more modest purpose of gaining for it understanding and respect. For the rest of us, such dialogue means getting past our prejudices and learned responses to "religion" long enough to ask, in an open and sustained way, whether the Bible after all helps us understand ourselves and helps us live more meaningfully in contemporary culture.

NOTES

Introduction

1. See *The Fundamentalists*, ed. R. A. Torrey, 4 vols. (Grand Rapids: Baker, 2003).

1. Why Any Educated Person Should Know the Bible

1. Ernesto Cardenal, *Psalms* (New York: Crossroad, 1981), 7. The classic exponent of this approach is Teilhard de Chardin, who incorporates the history of religion into a teleological vision of the total evolution of the cosmos.

2. Georg Büchner, *Werke und Briefe* (Leipzig: Insel, 1952), 171.

4. The Bible in Dialogue with a Pluralistic World

1. See the beneficially sober interpretation of his poetry by Eudo Colecesta Mason, *Rainer Maria Rilke: sein Leben und sein Werk*, Kleine Vandenhoeck-Reihe 192–94 (Göttingen: Vandenhoeck & Ruprecht, 1964).

2. Even a more strictly text-centered exegesis of the Gospel of John must conclude that its claim for exclusivity has two sides. In John, Christ is the light that is in all things and the Word that gives all things meaning (John 1:1-18). He is the bread and the light of the world, because the world at all times receives its life from him. Christ sends the Spirit as his successor. The Spirit will guide into all truth—even beyond what Jesus could say to his disciples (16:12-13). This Spirit, like the wind, blows where it will (3:8), giving free access to God without reference to the cultic centers on Gerizim and in Jerusalem: "God is spirit, and those who worship him must worship in spirit and truth" (4:24). Therefore Jesus is the "Savior of the world" (4:42). The Johannine Christ therefore claims exclusivity because he is, as the Word, the omnipresent creative power of God and because the Paraclete embodies his universal power to save after his death. Therefore, the claim of exclusivity must also be read backwards: no one comes to the Father but through Jesus, but those who have come to the Father have come to God through this universal Christ. In

his inaugural vision, Isaiah thought he was seeing God, but in reality he saw Christ (12:41). We may therefore say: even in the immanent textual world of the Gospel of John, the claim of exclusivity is less "exclusive" than it first appears.

3. There is also the hermeneutical principle behind all exegesis, namely, that every text has its own value. Its value is grounded in the independent value of every individual—and that person's utterances must never be viewed simply as a tool for understanding other utterances. Even if we had read the New Testament authors only in the light of their own faith, our hermeneutical convictions would force us to free ourselves from this reading.

1. Everything in the New Testament points back to the historical Jesus. He belongs in the context of Judaism and is also one of the foundations of Christianity. Jesus links two religions. If we study the Old Testament only as a condition for understanding the New Testament, then we should treat the historical Jesus only as a condition for understanding belief in the saving Christ (Rudolf Bultmann's consistent position). But if the historical Jesus has his own independent value theologically as well as historically, we must also ascribe independent value to the Old Testament—as a basis for the intellectual and spiritual milieu of Jesus.

2. In Romans 4:23-24, Paul says of Abraham's faith (with reference to Gen. 15:6): "Now the words, 'it was reckoned to him,' were written not for his sake alone, but for ours also." Here the point is explicit: besides its value for Christians, Scripture has its own independent value for Abraham. In Romans 4, Abraham serves as an example of a fully justifying faith in the setting of the Old Testament. He does not have faith in Christ but, like Christians, in the God who overcomes death. Any assessment of the Old Testament solely on the basis of its value for the New Testament inevitably leads to a contradiction.

4. Joachim Jeremias, *The Parables of Jesus*, 2nd rev. ed. (New York: Scribner, 1972), 139.

5. From al-Bukhari, *Ijara* ("The Book of Leasing"), sections 8 and 9, cited on pp. 279–80 by Otto Spies, "Die Arbeiter im Weinberg (Mt 20,1–15) in islamischer Überlieferung," *Zeitschrift für die neutestamentliche Wissenschaft* 66 (1975): 279–83.

6. Friedrich Schleiermacher, *The Christian Faith* (Philadelphia: Fortress Press, 1976), §24.

INDEX OF ANCIENT TEXTS

INDEX OF NAMES AND SUBJECTS

The Unfolding Drama of the Bible
Fourth Edition

Bernhard W. Anderson

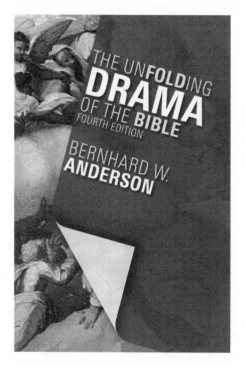

Religion / Bible
Paperback
120 pages
$13.00
ISBN 978-0-8006-3560-2

"Clear, accessible, reliable, up to date, and to the point. In a time of enormous biblical illiteracy, there is an acute need for guidance. In much church practice, moreover, there is a tendency to use isolated texts here and there, and so there is need for an overview that shows the whole picture of scripture in a coherent way. This brief articulation of 'the drama' meets those needs admirably."

—Walter Brueggemann
Columbia Theological Seminary

Faithful Interpretation
Reading the Bible in a Postmodern World

A. K. M. Adam

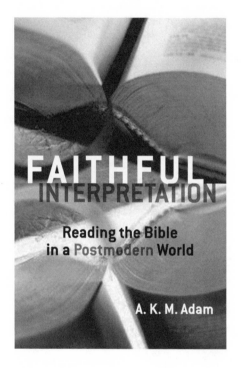

Religion / Biblical Studies
Paperback
208 pages
$20.00
ISBN 978-0-8006-3787-3

"Adam's analysis is critically acute and theologically edifying. Here is theological hermeneutics at its best."
— Stephen Fowl, Loyola College in Maryland

Engaging the Bible

Critical Readings from Contemporary Women

Edited by Choi Hee An and Katheryn Pfisterer Darr

Religion / Bible Interpretation
Paperback
208 pages
$20.00
ISBN 978-0-8006-3565-7

"This book is a treasure of focused illustrations, from many cultural perspectives, of how women's consciousness and creativity is transforming biblical interpretation and thus human society."

— Carolyn Osiek, Brite Divinity School

Constantine's Bible

Politics and the Making of the New Testament

David L. Dungan

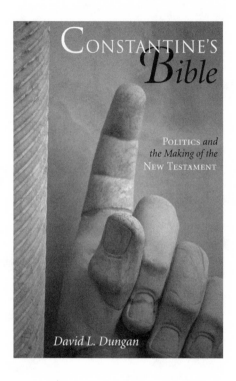

Religion / New Testament /
History of Religion
Paperback
240 pages
$17.00
ISBN 978-0-8006-3790-3

Most college and seminary courses on the New Testament include discussions of the process that gave shape to the New Testament. Now David Dungan re-examines the primary source for this history, the Ecclesiastical History of the fourth-century Bishop Eusebius of Caesarea, in the light of Hellenistic political thought. He reaches startling new conclusions.